A Tale
of Two Policies

A Tale of Two Policies

U.S. Relations with the Argentine Junta, 1976-1983

Mark Falcoff

FOREIGN POLICY RESEARCH INSTITUTE
Philadelphia
1989

Library of Congress Cataloging-in-Publication Data

Falcoff, Mark.
    A tale of two policies : U.S. relations with the Argentine junta,
1976-1983 / by Mark Falcoff.
        p.   cm. — (The Philadelphia papers)
    ISBN 0-910191-10-7
    1. United States—Foreign relations—Argentina.   2. Argentina—
Foreign relations—United States.   3. Argentina—Politics and
government—1955-1983.   4. United States—Foreign
relations—1977-1981.   5. United States—Foreign relations—1981-
I. Title. II. Series.
E183.8.A7F34   1989
327.73082—dc19   89-1552
                                                            CIP

Foreign Policy Research Institute
3615 Chestnut Street
Philadelphia, Pa. 19104

To Lawrence W. Levine
a good friend of Argentina
and of the author,
In appreciation

Contents

Foreword by Ambassador Frank Ortiz ... ix

Preface ... xi

I. **THE PARAMETERS OF U.S.-ARGENTINE RELATIONS** ... 1
Argentine Attitudes toward the United States ... 3
Argentina in the Inter-American System ... 5
Argentine Politics ... 6

II. **ARGENTINE POLITICS, 1946-1980** ... 9
What was Peronism? ... 9
The Search for a Post-Peronist Consensus ... 11
Peron's Second Coming and After ... 14
The Military Returns ... 15

III. **THE HUMAN RIGHTS ISSUE: ARGENTINA AS A POLICY PARADIGM, 1976-1981** ... 17
The Carter Administration: A Mixed Legacy ... 17
The Emergence of a Human Rights Policy ... 19
Why Argentina? ... 20
Carter Rethinks ... 22

IV. **ARGENTINA BECOMES A DOMESTIC POLITICAL ISSUE** ... 27
Argentina Becomes an Issue ... 27
Congress Takes a Hand ... 31

V. **AN ARGENTINE-AMERICAN ALLIANCE, 1981-82** ... 37
Where Was Argentina Heading, 1980-1982? ... 37
"At an Optimal Level": Bilateral Relations, 1981-1982 ... 42
The Slippery Path to Decline, November 1981-April 1982 ... 45

VI. **ARGENTINA GOES TO WAR** ... 49

VII. **CONCLUSIONS, AND SOME MIGHT-HAVE-BEENS** ... 55

Index ... 59

Foreword

For those who know and care about Argentina, the modern history of that nature-blessed land is often a subject of head-shaking fascination. In a foreign-service career spanning almost four decades, I have met no people who challenged my skills more than did the Argentines. And, even at this writing, I find no events more inexplicable than those that sometimes occur between the River Plate and the Andes. I and many others ought to be grateful to Mark Falcoff for easing at least some of our confusion in this fine study.

Dr. Falcoff deals in detail with the events of a ten-year period that had important effects on U.S.-Argentine relations. These were difficult years, as were the ones immediately preceding them. I remember well the convoluted and torturous negotiations to arrange a meeting at Camp David between President Juan Perón and the president of the United States in 1974. Both sides hoped this dialogue would open a new chapter in bilateral relations, but the meeting never materialized; Perón's health failed and he died shortly thereafter.

Developing the bilateral relationship soon became secondary as both the American and Argentine constitutional systems endured severe strains. In our own country, sturdy institutions carried us through the Watergate crisis. But in Argentina there was a descent into terrorist violence, violation of the constitution, pitiless state repression, economic failure, and then disastrous military adventurism.

Obsession with Argentina's volatile past threatens to obscure the signposts that might point the way to a more stable future. As Dr. Falcoff shows, the basic social, legal, and governmental institutions of Argentina emerged from the years of military rule weakened but in place. There is a democracy today in Argentina and one whose strength and stability, we hope, will grow. The United States should, and doubtlessly will, try to help, but if the past is any guide, U.S. relations with Argentina will again be marked periodically by promising vistas, exaggerated expectations and quick descents into disillusion.

There will remain, as always, a wary determination to achieve a mutually beneficial relationship. That determination has brought our bilateral relations to what might be their most realistic and hopeful level in recent times. The development of Argentina's bilateral relations with the leading democratic countries, particularly the United States, could be of special significance in setting the course of future events. Surely, the steady interest on the part of both Americans and Argentines to know one another better bodes well for the future. Already many long-standing misperceptions have been corrected, and new direct relationships have been established. The chances are bright that our two nations will at last stand alongside each other amidst the brotherhood of democratic nations, the best hope for the future of mankind.

Frank Ortiz
U.S. Ambassador to Argentina
1983-86

Preface

This book addresses an issue fundamental to both U.S.-Latin American relations and to American foreign policy generally—the rise and fall of the Argentine junta (1976-1983), its relations with the Carter and Reagan administrations, and the impact of each administration on successive military governments in Buenos Aires. It examines the specific to illuminate the general, in this case, the relationship between democratic (or non-democratic) institutions in Latin America and the role played by the U.S. government in the political evolution of its southern neighbors.

The larger topic is one about which there is, by now, a vast amount of literature of varying degrees of sophistication. In Latin America itself, where introspection and self-criticism are not highly developed arts, the dominant tradition has long been one of blaming others for national shortcomings. Since the dénouement of the Vietnam War and the fall of the Allende regime in Chile, some Americans have been eager to accept this culpability, and what was once a purely Latin American phenomenon has passed into public discourse in the United States. In its crudest and most common form, it holds that non-democratic governments owe their existence to Washington. Conversely, representative institutions only appear when the Central Intelligence Agency, the Pentagon, and the State Department have been asleep at the wheel. Both notions make frequent appearances in the op-ed pages of the prestige press, in university classrooms, and in Catholic and mainstream Protestant pulpits.

In a certain way this worldview is difficult to disprove. Democracy has not been the historical norm in Latin America. In contrast to its attitude in every other part of the globe, the United States has extended diplomatic recognition to nearly every Latin American government, whatever its politics. It has naturally looked with favor on those who proclaim themselves allies, and kept a certain distance from those who declare themselves adversaries. Almost all Latin American governments—whether democratic or not—have their differences with the United States; those that disappear violently or precipitately can always point retrospectively to some supposedly crucial policy difference with Washington as the presumptive reason to explain their misfortune.

Once the specifics of any case are examined in detail, however, the relationship between governments proves to be something less than simple and direct. That much is evident from the subject of this book. The dictatorship under review spanned two U.S. administrations that pursued diametrically opposed policies, neither of which worked as intended. The Carter administration's economic and military sanctions failed to deflect the junta from its course, and the Reagan administration's policy of "quiet diplomacy," which led to the de facto Argentine-American alliance of 1981-82, had an outcome neither side intended nor desired. If anything, the Argentine case illustrates the limits of American hegemony in a region long thought to be within its sphere of influence, Washington's ambivalence toward Latin allies, and the primacy of domestic rather than external forces in bilateral relationships such as these.

This study had its origins in a paper prepared for a conference on "Friendly Tyrants" at Chestnut Hill, Pennsylvania, in June 1987, sponsored by the Foreign Policy Research Institute. Both Dr. Daniel Pipes, director of the Institute, and his associate, Dr. Adam Garfinkle, invited me to expand my original paper so that it could be included in FPRI's monograph series, *The Philadelphia Papers*. I hasten to express my appreciation to them and to the Institute for this vote of confidence, and to my research assistant, Ricardo Maxit, for generating additional materials that enriched an already very interesting story.

Washington, D.C.
August 1988

The Parameters
of U.S.-Argentine Relations

Any study of bilateral relations normally begins with a review of the factors that bind two countries together, often in spite of great differences in history, culture, and levels of development. But in the case of the United States and Argentina, it is more productive to emphasize those elements that have divided both nations, since these have shaped and conditioned the relationship to an overwhelming degree.

Geography alone is a formidable barrier, even in the age of jet travel. Buenos Aires is nearly eleven hours' flying time from New York, roughly the same as Moscow; eight hours from Miami; fourteen hours (with a stopover in Lima) from Los Angeles. Moreover, the Argentine capital is not on the way to anywhere Americans normally go, unless they are planning an expedition to the Antarctic, or intending to continue on Eastern Airlines' regular daily flight to Santiago, Chile. Most of the airlines fly overnight, and the fares are roughly double those charged to major West European capitals.

The distance in statute miles works as a geographical metaphor for the still larger gap represented by economic, cultural, and political factors. There are, of course, some superficial similarities, particularly the fact that both nations are essentially new countries of the nineteenth century settled by immigrants. But unlike the United States, Argentines are largely descended from Italians and Spaniards, most of whom settled in Buenos Aires and other cities of the country's eastern littoral between 1880 and 1930. Though the architects of modern Argentina did envision agricultural settlement somewhat along the lines of the United States, the most productive land was already concentrated in a few hands by the time most immigrants arrived. Thus, Argentina is a frontier nation only in metaphor; its development as a modern society has been urban and, to a large degree, megacephalic, with the capital overshadowing and, in the view of many, exploiting an underpopulated interior.[1]

---

[1] This theme has been most convincingly explored in Ezequiel Martínez Estrada, *X-Ray of the Pampa*, trans. Alain Swetlecki (Austin: University of Texas Press, 1971). This long, somewhat convoluted essay, originally written in 1933, remains the best introduction to Argentine life and culture.

Both countries began as large-scale exporters of agricultural products and raw materials. But Argentina has largely persisted in that role, dependent upon shrinking and problematic foreign markets. The result has been an economy competitive with that of the United States, but under distinctly disadvantageous conditions since Argentina lacks the industrial and technological base to provide a defense-in-depth during periods of declining prices for agricultural products. An antiquated educational system, decimated by successive political purges and starved of resources, has forced the country to import most of its technology. Much of what industry Argentina has developed since 1930 is due to foreign investment, particularly (though not exclusively) from the United States. In 1977, for instance, American exposure was estimated at $1.5 billion,[2] the most visible foreign economic presence in the country and the source of much resentment across the Argentine political spectrum.

Historically, markets for Argentine exports were in Western Europe, particularly Great Britain. Most of the country's livestock are British breeds, sent out in the late nineteenth century; the British built the first meat-packing houses and railroads, and controlled most shipping and insurance up to the Second World War. Local political figures publicly referred to their country as "the sixth dominion" and, as one historian has written, as late as 1944 Argentina "remained one of the few areas in the world where English capital appeared to retain a secure foothold."[3]

Argentina began to trade extensively with the United States after the First World War, but the balances were always negative and had to be cleared in hard currency earned elsewhere, primarily in Europe. A unique triangularity characterized the Argentine-West European-U.S. commercial relationship, requiring for its successful operation the free flow of goods, services, shipping, and currencies. The Second World War and the development of the European Economic Community first disrupted then destroyed the conditions upon which these complicated arrangements rested. Since the early 1950s, Western Europe has been gradually replaced by the Soviet Union as Argentina's principal market for cereal exports, but the basic triangularity of U.S.-Argentine commerce has remained, as has its sharply asymmetrical dimensions; in 1975 the Argentine trade deficit with the United States was a record $431 million.[4]

---

[2] James Wilkie and Peter Reich, eds., *Statistical Abstract of Latin America, 1980* (Los Angeles: Center for Latin American Studies, University of California, Los Angeles, 1980), Table 3107.

[3] Harold Peterson, *Argentina and the United States* (Albany: State University of New York Press, 1964), p. 440.

[4] Edward Milenky, *Argentina's Foreign Policies* (Boulder: Westview Press, 1978), p. 109.

Argentine Attitudes Toward the United States

Argentina's relationship with Western Europe in the nineteenth and early twentieth centuries had important cultural corollaries that widened the gap between itself and the United States. A pervasive French influence among the intellectual class and the social elite produced a studied disdain for American culture and life, which sometimes blended imperceptibly into a repugnance for political democracy as such. The boundaries between left- and right-wing anti-Americanism in Argentina have never been well defined, and many different kinds of "anti-imperialists" have drunk indiscriminately at some of the same ideological wells. There has been much ideological cross-fertilization between Marxism, nationalism, fascism, and populism, with people switching parties and sides without ever abandoning their basic hostility to what they imagine to be the American way of life. For many Argentines, as for many West Europeans, the American way of life is envisioned as a combination of power, wealth, crassness, and crudity—an amalgam feared and envied at the same time.

At one time, Argentina regarded the United States in the spirit of friendly competition—as a rival with a similar destiny. Its founding fathers greatly admired the Puritan republic of the North (as they called it), and copied many features of its constitution for the Argentine charter of 1853, including the federal system. President Domingo Faustino Sarmiento (1868-1874), who had served as ambassador to the United States, was a frank enthusiast of all things American; he even imported schoolteachers from Boston to lay the foundations of the country's system of public education.

The process of estrangement between Argentina and the United States was gradual, and to some degree circumstantial. Trade and emigration patterns had much to do with it, as did the commercial and political rivalries of outsiders. The Germans cultivated Yankee-phobia in both world wars, and the local British community—the largest and most prosperous anywhere outside the Empire—sedulously promoted anti-Americanism as a response to the challenge posed to their monopoly of the meat-packing industry after the entry of Swift and Company in 1908.[5] In recent years, particularly since the 1950s, the country's economic performance has diverged so widely from that of the United States as to force many Argentines to seek consolation in illusions of cultural superiority.

The special relationship with Europe has also shaped Argentina's foreign policies, which have usually been neutralist and isolationist, both with respect to other Latin American countries as well as the

[5] Peter H. Smith, *Politics and Beef in Argentina: Patterns of Conflict and Change* (New York: Columbia University Press, 1969), pp. 57-81.

United States. As the late Arthur P. Whitaker once noted, "Argentina took no part in the Latin American congresses held at Panama in 1826 and at Lima in 1847 and 1864 for the purpose of establishing an inter-American security system, and rejected the Continental Treaty of 1856 drawn up by Chile, Peru, and Ecuador with the same end in view." Even when it subsequently laid a claim to the leadership of Latin America, "no effort was made to implement this through the establishment of a multilateral security system."[6]

The isolationist habit also explains in part Argentina's studied refusal to take sides during both world wars. But there were other factors present, as well. Though pro-German trends were present on both occasions, Argentina's policies were probably more inspired by the needs of the Allies, particularly Great Britain, for foodstuffs, which could only arrive safely on neutral bottoms. During the Second World War, under both civilian and military presidents, there was a stern conviction that the country's national interests "would best be served by a policy of prudent neutrality, since this would give her, a minor power, the maximum degree of security in the world-wide conflict of giants, and would enable her to extract the maximum advantage from it for her economy."[7]

There was, unquestionably, a decisive anti-American edge to Argentina's neutrality during the Second World War, though how much of it was inspired by sympathy for the Axis and how much by mere dislike for U.S. policies (or pretensions) can never be fully known.[8] In any case, what matters now are perceptions. Most Americans of a certain age can recall Argentina's refusal to join the United States at a moment of maximum peril; conversely, most Argentines of the same generation remember the rough-handed treatment accorded their aspirations for national sovereignty. Both latent grudges were revived—and at fever pitch—as recently as 1982, when the United States was compelled to take sides in an unexpected war between Argentina and Great Britain.

Likewise, commercial advantage—or necessity—rather than ideological preference determined Argentina's decision in 1979-1980 to ignore the grain embargo organized by the United States in the wake of the Soviet invasion of Afghanistan. Again, traditional anti-American themes and sentiments were present, as were specific grievances over President Carter's human rights policies; nonethe-

[6] Arthur P. Whitaker, *The United States and Argentina* (Cambridge: Harvard University Press, 1954), p. 87.

[7] Whitaker, ibid., p. 111.

[8] For contending versions see Cordell Hull, *Memoirs* (New York: Macmillan, 1948), vol. 2, pp. 1377-1419; and Sir David Kelly, *The Ruling Few* (London: Hollis and Carter, 1952), pp. 287-314. Kelly was British ambassador in Buenos Aires, 1942-46. For the objective evaluation of two historians, see Whitaker, *The United States and Argentina*, pp. 108-14; and Michael Francis, *The Limits of Hegemony: U.S. Relations with Argentina and Chile during World War II* (Notre Dame: University of Notre Dame Press, 1977), pp. 145-240.

less, given the crucial place that the Soviet Union now occupied in the Argentine economy, it is difficult to imagine how Buenos Aires might have seconded U.S. policies unless Washington had been willing to buy up the Argentine harvest for as much money or more.

Argentina in the Inter-American System

As noted above, Argentina has not been a particularly active player in the inter-American system, but to the degree that it has, it has striven to represent a pole of opposition to the United States. During the inter-war period it led the effort within the Pan American Union to exact a promise from the United States to abjure intervention in the internal affairs of Latin American republics. At the Panama Conference of the Pan American Union, it undermined the efforts of the United States to exact a clear-cut commitment by the Pan American states to break relations with the Axis in the event one of their number went to war with the latter. Though Argentina signed the Inter-American Treaty of Reciprocal Assistance (the Rio Pact) in 1947, and joined the new Organization of American States in 1948, these forums were used largely by President Juan Perón and his successors to criticize the United States or to oppose specific U.S. measures rather than to advance the cause of an inter-American consensus.

Under elected governments, Argentina has vigorously opposed U.S. efforts to introduce anti-communism into the inter-American system, or to interpret the security provisions of the Rio Pact to facilitate the containment of states that voluntarily opt into the Soviet bloc. Thus, Argentina opposed efforts to isolate Guatemala in 1954, and Cuba after 1959, and Nicaragua today. It broke relations with Castro only under enormous pressure from the United States, and restored them as soon as was practicable.[9] It also opted out of the trade embargo against Cuba originally imposed by the Organization of American States in 1973—this, under a military president, Lieutenant General Alejandro Lanusse, who had earlier proclaimed his acceptance of "ideological pluralism" at a historic meeting with Chilean Marxist president Salvador Allende in the northern city of Salta. More recently (1987), the government of President Raúl Alfonsín chose not to support a resolution critical of Cuban treatment of dissidents and political prisoners in the United Nations Commission on Human Rights, largely because it was sponsored by the United States. Normal relations with Cuba, complete with advantageous commercial relations with the Castro regime, have persisted under all Ar-

[9] For details, see Alberto A. Conil Paz and Gustavo Ferrari, *Argentina's Foreign Policy, 1930-62*, trans. John J. Kennedy (Notre Dame: University of Notre Dame Press, 1966), pp. 183-201.

gentine governments, including some military regimes that advertised themselves as ferociously anti-communist.

Argentine Politics

Argentina's problematic political life has added yet another negative dimension to the bilateral relationship. Since 1930, the country has experienced few prolonged periods of constitutional democracy. Democratic forms were respected between 1932-1943, but the elected governments of the day were delegitimized by electoral fraud. Argentina languished under direct military rule in 1943-46, 1955-58, 1962-63, 1966-1973, and 1976-1983, that is, for twenty-one out of forty years. General Juan Perón served as an elected president from 1946-1955, but governed in a semi-authoritarian style which led many to regard him as a dictator. Likewise, President Arturo Illia (1963-66) was widely (if somewhat unfairly) regarded as a front man for colonels, since his election was made possible only through the proscription of the largest political party in the country.

Thus, between 1930 and 1983—more than half a century—the only civilian chief of state elected freely and fairly, and who governed in strict adherence to democratic norms, was Arturo Frondizi (1958-1962). But he was able to obtain power in the first place only by concluding a pact with Perón (then living in exile in Venezuela) to legalize the Peronist party once in office. Perón then instructed his followers to vote for Frondizi. When the latter kept his end of the bargain, the Peronists swept provincial and congressional elections in 1962. The armed forces intervened and concluded Frondizi's presidency two years early. Under complicated rules then devised to exclude the Peronists from the ballot box, Dr. Arturo Illia, leader of a rival branch of the Radical party, limped into office the following year with 23 percent of the vote. He in turn was deposed in a coup three years later.

By the early 1970s, then, it was common in the United States to regard Argentina as a basically ungovernable country, destined to career back and forth between different kinds of military regimes, punctuated by an occasional weak civilian government. The one political alternative acceptable to the largest number of Argentines—a restoration of the Perón regime—was also unacceptable to at least 40 percent of the electorate.

From a foreign-policy perspective there was little for Washington to choose from, since all of the known political combinations—right-wing authoritarianism, populist gangsterism, or indecisive, unviable civilian rule—were more or less hostile to American values or international objectives. Writing in 1954, the year before Perón's fall, Arthur Whitaker cautioned Americans not to place excessive stock in the opposition Radical party. "All told," he said, "the Radicals go even beyond Perón in their Yankeephobia. He heaped unmeasured abuse upon the United States as a matter of tactics; their attacks on this country's policies, though less virulent, are based on principle."[10] And he correctly prophesied that "so long as the United States adheres to its present policies, the ousting of Perón would probably result not in an improvement but a deterioration of relations."[11]

As it turned out, the two elected civilian governments since 1930—Arturo Frondizi and Arturo Illia—were more congenial to the United States than the others, but this had no practical effect whatever. Neither man enjoyed a genuine political majority, both had run on political platforms promising punitive action against U.S. oil companies,[12] and both had opposed U.S. policies with regard to Cuba and the Dominican Republic. Illia himself made something of a fetish out of his opposition to what later came to be called multinational corporations, and actively sought confrontation with the United States over petroleum concessions and the sale of pharmaceuticals.[13]

The dilemma of Argentine domestic politics for U.S. foreign policy was captured in *The New York Times* lead story the day after Illia was overthrown by the armed forces on June 29, 1966. "The United States moved quickly today to express its disapproval of the military ouster of President Arturo U. Illia of Argentina, but appeared undecided over what, if anything, to do about it." At the time, the Johnson administration was deeply embroiled in negotiations over compensation to U.S. oil companies expropriated by the fallen government, and over the terms under which Argentina could nonetheless continue to receive aid under the Alliance for Progress. But the real key to Washington's indecision lay deeper in the same dispatch: "Apart from the effect of the declaration of a bank holiday, most Argentines went about their usual activities. In fact," it added, "the almost universal indifference of the populace to the fate of the democratic Government during its struggle with right-wing and left-wing opponents encouraged the military's actions."[14]

The United States could not make Argentina more democratic than Argentines wanted it to be, which the available evidence suggested was not very much. The issue of human rights abroad had yet to make its appearance in U.S. domestic politics, but even if it had, well up to 1976 it would have been difficult for most Americans—whether conservative or liberal, in government or outside it—to iden-

[10] Whitaker, *The United States and Argentina*, p. 251.
[11] Ibid., p. 252.
[12] Frondizi had even written an extended quasi-Marxist pamphlet, *Política y petróleo* (1954), identifying these as the root cause of all his country's political ills.
[13] While a man of considerable personal integrity, Illia was remarkably naive. To the day of his death in 1983 he was convinced that the military coup that brought about his fall nearly twenty years before had been caused by American pharmaceutical companies.
[14] H.J. Maidenberg, "Military Junta Ousts President in Argentina, Puts General in Charge," *The New York Times*, June 27, 1966.

tify political forces in Argentina that they could wholeheartedly support. This more than anything else explains why Argentina remained a distant player in U.S. Latin American policy for so many years, and why doubtless it would have remained so had it not been for new developments in both countries in the final half of the 1970s.

Argentine Politics
1946-1980

What was Peronism?

The fundamental drama of Argentine politics after Perón's fall in 1955 was the inability of the system to incorporate and supersede the experience of his nine years in office. Given the lasting impact of this period, a review of its principal characteristics is useful.

From some points of view, Perón was a truly revolutionary figure: he sponsored the creation of a massive trade union movement; he nationalized the Argentine railroads and other public services; he greatly expanded the public sector and government services; he (and his wife, Eva, who died in 1952) attacked frontally all of the styles and values of what passed for "high society," leveling distinctions of class, region and color, and social styles.[1] All of these things were done in a highly personal manner; the informing principle of Peronism was not ideology but loyalty to the leader (and while she lived, his wife). Nonetheless, they were profoundly upsetting to traditional Argentine politics.

Prior to Perón, public life in Argentina was dominated by three major political forces, with a potential fourth beginning to emerge. The first was an upper class of ranchers-cum-lawyers, represented by the National Democratic (that is, Conservative) party, with allies and affiliates in the small cities and towns of the interior, supported by the foreign business community and the Roman Catholic hierarchy. These groups could deliver not only their own votes, but those of their tenants, employees, servants, communicants, and other dependents. This was the political combination that had ruled Argentina during the "golden age" of the aristocracy (1880-1916), and made possible its development as a modern nation. Deposed by a suffrage reform in 1912, the Conservatives recaptured control of Argentine politics in 1930 by means of a military coup, and have provided most

---

[1] By "social styles" is meant customs such as requiring men to wear coats and ties in public places, including parks and other places of amusement.

9

of the civilian personnel of military governments in the years since 1955.

Leading the opposition was the middle-class Radical party, founded in the 1890s and eventually the victor in the first free and fair presidential election in 1916. During the 1920s, the Radicals came to think of themselves as a *partido único*—that is, harbingers of a one-party state, something along the lines of what later emerged in Mexico under the Partido Revolucionario Institicional (PRI). However, the Radicals' inability to generate new leadership, and their insistence upon re-nominating President Hipólito Yrigoyen in 1928 though he was nearly eighty and arguably senile, left the party helpless when the Depression devastated the country, affording the Conservatives and the army the excuse they were waiting for.

In addition, a third party, the small Socialist party, articulated the views of public employees, skilled workers, schoolteachers, professionals, and intellectuals generally. It had some influence on the intellectual climate, but little real political clout.

Finally, there was the Argentine Communist party. From the time of its founding in 1922, the party was subject to much police repression but, before Perón, it was nonetheless beginning to sink roots into the new industrial working class. That class, which came into existence in the 1930s, expanded greatly in size during the Second World War.

Perón's political genius led him to introduce an entirely new fracture-line in Argentine politics, splitting off important segments of each of the traditional political forces. From the Conservatives he took the church and most of the party's provincial affiliates, as well as the rural proletariat and servant class in its entirety; from the Radicals, he lured away ambitious politicians and professionals, businessmen, and the more nationalistic intellectuals; from the Socialists, he recruited several members of parliament and many labor leaders; from the Communists, much of their working-class constituency.

Not surprisingly, the coalition that had supported Perón's overthrow in 1955 was the remnant of the old regime that had resisted the Peronist wave in 1946.[2] It stretched from the Conservatives, who resented the substance of Perón's reforms, to Socialists and Radicals who might otherwise have supported his policies but who resented the undemocratic fashion in which he implemented them, or the evident corruption and arrogance of his associates, or the leader's high-handed treatment of his opposition.

---

[2] With the exception of right-wing Catholics, who changed sides once again in 1954 when Perón quarrelled with the Church over educational policy and divorce.

The Search for a Post-Peronist Consensus

Logically, then, the moment the great man disappeared from the scene, his successors began to quarrel among themselves. New elections were postponed for three more years while the armed forces and their closest civilian advisers dithered over how to reconstitute the political system. A new president and congress were finally chosen in 1958, but without resolving the fundamental problem. Every possible political combination in the years that followed—proscription of Peronism, "integration" into another movement (Frondizi), outright repression, or the "de-personalization" of the movement—failed in its purpose. While at no point could it be said that the Peronist Justicialist party represented a solid majority of voters, it never dropped below 30 percent and probably hovered for much of the late 1960s and early 1970s at 45 percent.[3] It thus remained the largest single bloc in Argentine politics.

Conceivably, this would not have been the case had the Argentine economy performed somewhat better than it did in the late 1950s and 1960s. As it was, as time went by people increasingly remembered the Peronist period as one of relative prosperity and economic growth. This required a bit of selective recollection, but was not totally at variance with the facts. The times in Argentina had indeed been good in the late 1940s; gold surpluses accumulated during the Second World War facilitated imports, and the high prices that agricultural products commanded in the immediate postwar period promoted considerable growth and prosperity. The country's economic decline actually began under Perón in the early 1950s, but deepened under his successors; this allowed his partisans to escape the blame for many unfortunate policies that actually began during the great man's second presidential term (1952-55). For example, mismanagement of agricultural resources during Perón's second administration forced the government to ration meat for the first time in the nation's history.

Argentina might also have moved on to other political choices had Perón himself been killed in the coup that overthrew him, or died of natural causes soon thereafter. As it was, he flourished in exile, first in Paraguay, then Panama, then Nicaragua, Venezuela, the Dominican Republic, and finally Spain, where he lived from January 1960 until his return to Buenos Aires in 1973. In exile he became a distant legend hovering over Argentine public life, his every pronouncement headline news, his state of health a burning topic of any political discussion. His redoubt in Madrid became an

---

[3] Perón's stand-in at the 1973 presidential elections, Héctor Cámpora, received 49 percent of the vote.

alternative pole of attraction for dissident politicians and intellectuals, many of whom had opposed him during his presidency in the 1940s, and for Argentine students living or traveling in Europe. Argentine politics had fallen to such a state that, by 1970, the real question was not whether he would return, but when and under what conditions.

An even more pregnant question was what Peronism would represent in its second coming. In the 1940s and 1950s, the left in Argentina had regarded Perón as a "fascist," even though his regime had strong populist, redistributionist, and "anti-imperialist" strains and thus enjoyed the support of the vast majority of Argentine workers. During the 1940s, Communists and assorted left-wing intellectuals convinced themselves that this was a classic case of "false consciousness"—that utterly arrogant notion that enables Marxist intellectuals to decide what is best for working people. But once Perón departed the scene they quickly discovered that his primary constituency, the trade unions, could not be coaxed to other ideologies and movements. By the late 1960s, the country's intellectual left and its student class were forced to rethink their attitude toward Peronism, and the rather bizarre way that they did so led to developments with far-reaching political consequences.

The revisionist mood was encouraged not merely by the dictates of expediency (Peronism remained, as it were, the only working-class political show in town), but by the example of the Cuban revolution. As the Argentine left chose to read events in Cuba, Castro had not been a Communist at the time of his revolutionary victory in 1959, but had stumbled into Marxism as the only possible solution to the problems of power and survival. That is, they theorized that the Cuban *caudillo* had counted his divisions once in power, discovered the Marxist left to be the largest and best-organized faction and immediately ran in front of them. Under the right circumstances, a new generation of Argentine Marxists argued, might not Perón be compelled to do the same thing?[4]

Gazing upon all this from his redoubt in Spain, Perón did nothing to discourage this line of thinking among a new generation of followers, although to his old-line associates he continued to speak approvingly of Benito Mussolini, Primo de Rivera, and others in the pre-Nazi Fascist pantheon. He repeatedly insisted and indeed no doubt believed that there really was no difference between Italian fascism and Third World socialism. As he explained it to me in Madrid in August 1968, his political philosophy was "the third position between capitalism and communism, that of two-thirds of humanity

---

[4] There are many versions of this "Trotsko-Peronism," or "Marxism *con poncho*," but the best-known and most influential are found in the writings of Jorge Abelardo Ramos and the late Rodolfo Puiggrós. Of particular interest is Ramos's *El partido comunista argentino: su historia y su crítica* (Buenos Aires: Coyoacán, 1962), and his journal, *Izquierda Nacional*, which appeared fitfully in the late 1960s.

today, from the Scandinavian Social Democrats . . . to the emerging nations of Africa and Asia."

This sudden fusion of ideological categories, combined with the determination of a new generation of Argentine leftists to express themselves through direct action, led to nearly a decade of political violence. Between 1968 and 1973 Perón destroyed Argentina's military government by encouraging others to embark upon robberies, kidnappings, and murders, in which favored targets were the military or their (real or perceived) allies in the business community, particularly executives of American companies. These episodes served to demoralize Argentina's military rulers and their civilian allies, and to hasten the day when the service chiefs would decide upon political devolution. Meanwhile, Perón insisted that he had not changed at all; that the events in Argentina were merely the logical response of a frustrated generation whose concerns needed to be channeled along constructive lines. This was Perón's way of telling conservative and moderate elements that he alone could restore the country's prosperity and social peace.

Thus, by 1972 there were two versions of Peronism available to Argentines: one preaching revolution and practicing revolutionary violence, another promising the restoration of order, prosperity, and traditional values. One side, whose vanguard was a Marxist urban guerrilla movement and most of whose members were new converts to Peronism, had as its battle-cry *"La patria socialista."*[5] The other, drawn from old-line supporters or their children, led by populist-nationalists or right-wing Catholics who had returned to the fold,[6] called for "La patria justicialista"—that is, a return to the regime they had known in the late 1940s. Underestimating this rising tide, or perhaps merely its capacity to join two such disparate elements into a coherent movement, the military continued to play for time, until elections could no longer be postponed. Even then they wrote the election rules in such a way that Perón himself would be ineligible to run.

But Perón outwaited and outwitted the generals. He designated a colorless subordinate of unquestioned loyalty, Héctor J. Cámpora, to stand for the presidency in his stead; Cámpora handily defeated Radical party candidate Ricardo Balbín and was inaugurated on May 25, 1973. Once Cámpora was firmly installed in office, he was ordered to Madrid and told to resign; this he did on July 13, turning over the seals of office to a provisional president, Raul Lastiri, pledged to

[5] For a very useful discussion of this phenomenon, which Juan José Sebreli calls "fascismo de izquierda" (left-wing fascism), see his *Los deseos imaginarios del peronismo* (Buenos Aires: Editorial Legasa, 1983). Among other things, he shows how many urban guerrilla leaders began their careers in Argentina's fascistoid right.

[6] Perón made peace with the Church in the early 1960s and was readmitted to communion.

convoke new presidential elections in September. In those elections, Perón was pitted against Balbín, and defeated him with 60 percent of the vote.

Perón's Second Coming and After

The calculated contradictions that made possible Perón's return to power began to unravel the moment he stepped on Argentine soil on June 20, 1973. As his jet neared the landing strip at Ezeiza International Airport, the leaders of both wings of his movement—left and right, old-guard and Marxist converts—confronted one another in a vain attempt to seize control of the podium and ensure that "their" Perón was the one who had returned. A shoot-out resulted in the death of dozens of people; uncounted others were wounded, or abducted and tortured in the airport hotel in rooms specially reserved for this purpose. Shocked at news of the disorder, Perón ordered his plane diverted to a military airfield, and from there proceeded to a residence in the suburbs of Buenos Aires, where he went into a month's seclusion.

From the moment of Perón's return it was evident that he had no intention of really changing his political colors. Cámpora and his vice president were not merely ordered to resign; there was a wholesale purge of their administration, eliminating leftists and others who were suspected of having ties to the urban guerrillas. Marxist infiltration was particularly evident at the Ministry of Interior, the federal agency in charge of the police and judiciary, which during Cámpora's brief period of office had issued a wholesale amnesty for terrorists captured, tried, and convicted during the early 1970s.

The Peronist left viewed these developments with apprehension, but refused to admit that it had misjudged its leader. During the month of July, it met almost continuously at the cell, district, regional, and national levels, trying to devise a means to set the agenda of Perón's third presidency. Much attention was given to the choice of his running mate, since the great man himself was seventy-nine years old, in precarious health, and evidently unlikely to survive the impending six-year term. One name that continually surfaced in left-wing circles was Augusto Tosco, a union leader from Córdoba who, unlike most Peronist trade union secretaries, spoke and thought like a Marxist.

Tosco never had a chance. Perón demonstrated that he was still firmly in charge at the end of the month, when he designated his third wife, María Estela Martínez de Perón ("Isabel") to be his running mate. Apart from the fact that Señora Perón lacked the requisite political experience—enough so to cause any Argentine to draw a deep breath—to the extent that anything was known about her political views, she was identified with the traditionalist wing of the party. The left was given the choice of accepting Perón (and Isabel) on his own terms or leaving his movement altogether.

This it did in the following year, in a dramatic public confrontation at the Plaza de Mayo in Buenos Aires. Accepting Perón's challenge, the formations of the left angrily marched out of a huge public demonstration of support for the president, now old and ailing, but still the supreme leader. Soon the same sort of violence that had been inflicted upon Perón's enemies was launched against him and his supporters; after Perón's death in July 1974, the conflict escalated into a civil war in miniature—between urban guerrillas on one hand and the armed forces of the government they had helped to install on the other.

President Isabel Perón was even less capable than her husband of mastering the complexities of the political and military situation, and she relied heavily upon others for advice. One of the personalities closest to the new president was the minister for social welfare, José López Rega. A former police corporal and bodyguard for Perón during his presidency in the 1940s, López Rega had come to the attention of Señora Perón during a visit to Argentina in 1964; thereafter he moved to Spain, assuming duties as Perón's private secretary, confidant, and general factotum. A sinister figure who dabbled in astrology, López Rega was also widely rumored to be linked to the Argentine Anti-Communist Alliance (the so-called Triple A), a paramilitary movement with close ties to the police, to the extreme right wing of the Peronist party, and to the labor movement. The paramilitary right was part of Buenos Aires's murky underworld, in which politics, crime, trade-union racketeering, and an occasional clerical intrigue met and intermingled. Under López Rega's influence, civil-military conflict in Argentina became a three-sided affair, in which various parties and the armed forces worked together or at cross-purposes, as circumstances ordained.

The Military Returns

Between 1974 and 1976, the Argentine government was both a victim and perpetrator of terror. Buenos Aires and other major cities became virtual battlegrounds, particularly at night. When the armed forces assumed power on March 25, 1976, it was to the visible relief of large segments of the population. Beneath the superficial veneer of normality, however, the civil war merely entered a new and uglier phase. Between 1976 and 1978 the Argentine military managed to liquidate the terrorists and their accomplices, but in the process they abducted and murdered many others guilty of no crime other than militance in left-wing political movements or intellectual circles, or merely of being an acquaintance of someone who was. A characteristic technique of the dragnet was to seize people's personal address books and systematically interrogate or abduct people inscribed therein.

More than a decade later, and despite intensive investigations after the fact, it is still difficult to fix the precise dimensions of the "dirty war." Estimates of the number of persons who died as victims of terrorist attacks vary widely, from a low of 500 to an upper estimate of 2,500; a national commission appointed in 1983 to look into disappearances at the hands of the armed forces, paramilitary organizations, or allied civilian shock groups took depositions on behalf of 9,000 persons.[7]

By 1979 Argentina was still under a state of seige, but a semblance of normality was returning. There were still occasional disappearances; some 900 persons were still held at the disposition of the executive power (equivalent to arrest without *habeas corpus*); political activity was still forbidden. In late 1980, President General Jorge Videla stepped down in favor of army commander General Roberto Viola, who was installed for a four-year term beginning in March 1981.

Though little was known of Viola's political views, there were indications that he had ties to sectors of the political community, and also that he planned to preside more effectively over the government and defer less to the judgment of his colleagues on the ruling junta. In other words, it was expected that he would rule somewhat more in the quasi-civilian style of Argentina's pre-1976 military presidents. The fact that he had retired from active service before assuming office was regarded as a hopeful sign, as was his rather low-key personal style.

Some political leaders, particularly Peronists, were anxious to put the best possible face on the change of guard at the Casa Rosada, Argentina's White House. Thus, Viola's first major speech received enthusiastic reviews from Felipe Deolindo Bittel, first vice president of the Peronist party, who said that it opened "favorable prospects for the Argentine people. This is our way of talking," he added, "and with that kind of language we are going to understand each other."[8] The next day the new interior minister qualified Peronism as a "valid interlocutor" in any future government dialogue with the parties, this despite its still being officially proscribed.[9] This is where matters stood in Argentina when, amid much anticipation there and in the United States, Ronald Reagan assumed the presidency.

---

[7] National Commission on Disappeared Persons (CONADEP), *Nunca más* (New York: Pantheon Books, 1986).

[8] Foreign Broadcast Information Service—*Latin America*, April 8, 1981 (hereafter referred to as FBIS—*LAT*, and the corresponding date.)

[9] Ibid.

The Human Rights Issue: Argentina as a Policy Paradigm, 1976-1981

The Carter Administration: A Mixed Legacy

Nine months after the Argentine military deposed Isabel Perón, a new administration took office in the United States committed to revise almost all of the trends of postwar foreign policy.[1] The Carter dispensation represented the confluence of several themes that had been growing in importance since the mid-1960s, and reached a sort of generational flood tide by 1976. Together they led human rights to become, for the first time, the bedrock of American foreign policy.

One of these principles was the eradication of racial injustice, to be led by reconstructed white Southerners like the new president himself, but now projected outward on a global scale. Several key members of the Carter team, particularly the new assistant secretary of state for human rights and humanitarian affairs, Patricia Derian, came from the same background as the president, experienced a similar transformation, and shared the same worldview; others, like United Nations Ambassador Andrew Young, frankly and boldly saw foreign policy as little more than an extension of their earlier civil rights work.[2]

Another principle was a repugnance for anti-communism and military intervention overseas, viewed as parts of an inseparable Cold War whole. This was matched by a pervasive sense of shame for the allies the United States had chosen and supported in times past and the need to bring foreign policy in line with U.S. domestic political and cultural values, and also with what Carter perceived as a declining Soviet threat. As the president put it in one of his earliest major foreign-policy statements:

[1] For a sympathetic review, see George D. Moffett III, *The Limits of Victory* (Ithaca: Cornell University Press, 1985), especially pp. 48-70.

[2] "Playboy Interview: Andrew Young," *Playboy*, July 1977, pp. 61-83.

We are now free of that inordinate fear of communism which once led us to embrace any dictator who joined us in that fear . . . .

For too many years, we've been willing to adopt the flawed and erroneous principles and tactics of our adversaries, sometimes abandoning our own values for theirs. We've fought fire with fire, never thinking that fire is better quenched with water. This approach failed, with Vietnam the best example of its intellectual and moral poverty . . . .

Referring to postwar American foreign policy, Carter went on to say that:

Historical trends have weakened its foundation. The unifying threat of conflict with the Soviet Union has become less intensive . . . .

The world is still divided by ideological disputes, dominated by regional conflicts, and threatened by danger that we will not resolve the differences of race and wealth without violence or without drawing into combat the major military powers.

But, he added:

We can no longer separate the traditional issues of war and peace from the new global questions of justice, equity, and human rights.[3]

In other words, the United States had erred because it had misjudged the real issues facing humanity, and in so doing, had found itself in disreputable company—as if that, and not other military, strategic, and political considerations led to U.S. defeat in Vietnam. While Carter admitted that certain strategic and ideological considerations were still operative, he saw the international environment as changing in ways that would allow the United States to compete more advantageously in the area of values and of example.

A third central principle was morality in public life. This was informed by the president's own deep religious convictions, which he displayed prominently, and nurtured by broad public apprehension over the misdeeds of high public officials during the late 1960s and early 1970s. Revelations of U.S. involvement in plots to assassinate foreign leaders, the fall of the Allende government in Chile, pay-offs to the vice president of the United States, and finally, the Watergate scandal itself gave rise to a strong sense within the Carter administration, rarely articulated as such but frequently implicit in public statements by the president and other high officials, that the United States had best put its own house in order before reading lessons to others. At the same time, however, and somewhat paradoxically, there was an equally strong conviction that one way to purge ourselves of past sins at home would be to proceed according to a higher moral standard in our policies abroad.

[3] "University of Notre Dame, Address at Commencement Exercises of the University, May 22, 1977," *Public Papers of the Presidents: Jimmy Carter*, Vol. 1 (Washington, D. C.: GPO, 1978), pp. 956-57.

The Emergence of a Human Rights Policy

The human rights policy itself had an honorable beginning as a protest against the *Realpolitik* of the Nixon and Ford administrations, or, as some would have it, the foreign policy of Henry A. Kissinger. The ubiquitous secretary of state regarded as fundamental the need to reach a new understanding with the Soviet Union and China, for which purpose humanitarian issues, along with a great many other important considerations, were placed on the back burner. Many Americans were frankly shocked at the way Kissinger spoke disdainfully of political figures who insisted on raising such inconvenient issues as the plight of Soviet Jews;[4] in areas more peripheral to his interests, such as South America, "soft" policies (or even some "hard" ones), claimed little or none of his attention or interest.[5]

By the mid-1970s, human rights was an issue that arguably appealed to a broad spectrum of American opinion. Largely due to public and congressional pressure, the Ford administration created the position of coordinator for human rights at the State Department, later elevated by the Carter administration to the position of assistant secretary. By placing human rights at the top of the foreign-policy agenda, the 1976 Democratic platform was also able to unite two somewhat contradictory currents within the party—the traditional, anti-Soviet conservatives, centered in the labor movement, the Jewish community, and a minority of the intellectual class; and a "new politics" constituency made up of intellectuals, media and entertainment people, young professionals, teachers, veterans of the civil rights movement, and repentant Cold Warriors traumatized by the Vietnam War and the coup in Chile.

But the Carter administration had not been in office a year before it stumbled against the outer limits of morality in foreign policy. Human rights was virtually withdrawn from the U.S.-Soviet agenda after Secretary of State Cyrus Vance's initial visit to Moscow in March 1977, where the Soviets made it forcefully clear that such importunities endangered the future of arms control, and indeed, the whole bilateral relationship.[6] An initial decision to punish South Korea for its frequent mistreatment of its own domestic opposition by drawing down the U.S. troop presence there was quickly reversed as the result of pressure from Congress, the Defense Department, and several allied Asian countries.[7] While the decision to back down in each case may have been right and proper from the point of view

---

[4] Such as the late senator Henry Jackson, whom Kissinger repeatedly characterized as a "politician running for President," as if that in itself were a damning epithet.

[5] Kissinger's own version is, of course, somewhat different. See *Years of Upheaval* (Boston: Little, Brown, 1982), pp. 410-13, 988.

[6] Joshua Muravchik, *The Uncertain Crusade* (Lanham: Hamilton Press, 1986), pp. 23-24.

[7] South Korea was, however, treated much as Argentina and Chile at the international financial institutions; the United States always voted against its loan proposals.

of the U.S. national interest, it forced the administration either to abandon its human rights policy altogether or apply it selectively.

Having explicitly raised the issue in the 1976 elections, created a new human rights bureaucracy at the State Department, and boldly proclaimed a new agenda for American foreign policy, the Carter people had no choice but to opt for the second course. The organizing principle of human rights policy became not the degree of repression in an individual country, but its ideological orientation—to the general benefit of "socialist" countries;[8] its foreign policy—manifesting a passive preference for "neutralist" Third World dictatorships; and the judgment—casual or informed, as the case might have been—of Assistant Secretary Patricia Derian as to how much of a difference U.S. pressures and sanctions could make.[9] In practice this meant that the Philippines and Chile were treated more harshly than Yugoslavia or Romania, but also more harshly than such egregious offenders as Syria, Iraq, Panama, Algeria, Somalia, and Guineau-Bissau.[10]

Why Argentina?

On the sheer merits of the case, there was certainly no reason *not* to have a human rights policy for Argentina; by any standard, it deserved to figure near the top of any list of target countries, particularly in 1977 and 1978. The problem arose when it became evident that not facts alone, but certain political and ideological considerations were guiding administration human rights policy, undermining its claims to objectivity and universality. The disproportionate energy applied to Argentina (and Nicaragua) was intended, apparently, to compensate for lack of zeal elsewhere. Here, after all, was a country with a long history of hostility to the United States in which there was no evident and obvious countervailing security interest, and in which the rulers represented (or were perceived to represent) everything the Carter people despised, from anti-communism to anti-Semitism, from monetarism to militarism. To make the brew even more piquant, because of its close commercial rela-

[8] President Carter even publicly declared on a visit to Poland in 1977 that he was satisfied with the human rights situation there, a remark that justifiably unleashed the full fury of both the liberal left and the conservative right in the United States. For the text, see *Public Papers of the Presidents: Jimmy Carter, 1977*, Vol. 2 (Washington, D.C.: GPO, 1978), pp. 2208-09.

[9] She often remarked that while the Soviet autocracy was wholly regrettable, there was nothing the United States could do about *that*. Better to apply ourselves, she would say, to those areas where we could effect a positive change, such as Argentina. (Evidence to me of a career foreign service officer who served on her staff, and wishes to remain anonymous.)

[10] Muravchik, *The Uncertain Crusade*, pp. 125-26. Since one of the major foreign-policy goals of the Carter administration was to win ratification of two treaties returning the canal to Panama, irregularities in that country were promptly swept under the rug. Conversely, conservative senators, not normally kept awake at night by human rights violations in Latin America, suddenly discovered the exquisite pleasures of "caring," adding a fun-house dimension to the debate over ratification.

tionship with the Soviet Union, there was a species of Argentine-Soviet entente on such matters as human rights. At the International Labor Organization in Geneva, the two normally supported one another against critics whenever repression of labor movements was on the agenda.[11]

The Carter human rights policy was applied to Argentina in five different ways. First, there were frequent public denunciations by the president, by his aides, and by the State Department of human rights violations, particularly the persistence of thousands of "disappeared" persons. Second, under the Humphrey-Kennedy Amendment to the Foreign Assistance Act (1976), an embargo was placed upon the sale of arms and spare parts to Argentina (and Chile), or the training of its military personnel. Third, the United States consistently voted against Argentine loan requests at the multilateral development banks. Fourth, the United States refused Export-Import Bank financing for Argentine purchases in the United States. Fifth, the United States consistently supported resolutions against Argentina at the United Nations Commission on Human Rights.

By 1980 it was possible to draw up a balance sheet on the effectiveness of these actions. On the positive side, entire sectors of the Argentine public normally predisposed to believe the worst about the United States were suddenly shocked into the realization that there was no necessary relationship between the presence of a large U.S. business community in the country, and support by Washington or the local embassy for military repression. Many professional "anti-imperialists," particularly those whose families were the beneficiaries of U.S. official intervention, were forced to revise their notions about the United States as a political culture and a force in the world.

By persistence and the sheer allocation of policy energy, the Carter White House and State Department were able to win the release of several important political prisoners, most notably newspaper publisher Jacobo Timerman. It is even arguable that the sheer scale and horror of the "dirty war" against real or imagined enemies of national security would have been far worse had not the United States acted as it did. Nonetheless, virtually the totality of the 9,000 victims disappeared during the period when the Carter policy was being applied.

On a more mundane level, U.S. sanctions had little or no impact on Argentina's economy or military preparedness. In no case did U.S.

[11] During this period the Soviet press and the Argentine Communist party spoke rather equivocally of the military regime; as late as 1981, party spokesman Rubens Iscaro told a Cuban journalist that there were several different strains within the military government, suggesting that some were more "positive" than others. The main enemy was what he called "Pinochetism," against which the party had been fighting. "The danger of a fascist dictatorship cannot be ignored." However, he added, "so far fascism has been unsuccessful." *Yearbook of International Communist Affairs, 1983* (Stanford: Hoover Institution Press, 1983), p. 56.

votes in the multilateral lending institutions deprive it of credits, and whatever could not be obtained from concessionary financing could easily be obtained from private banks in the United States, Western Europe, or Japan. Thus, between 1976 and 1980, the Argentine foreign debt increased from US$8.9 billion to US$27.2 billion, a record increase in both real and relative terms.[12] As for the arms embargo, long before the Carter administration Argentina's military leaders had been seeking to diversify their dependency on foreign services. They had succeeded to the extent that, by 1976, only about a third of all military acquisitions originated in the United States; the others came from France, West Germany, Canada, Israel, South Africa, Taiwan, or from Argentina's own expanding National Directorate of Military Factories (DNFM).[13] With other suppliers rushing in to absorb the portion that the United States had voluntarily relinquished, National Security Adviser Zbigniew Brzezinski was led to remark, "If we exercise restraint but other nations do not, nothing much has been gained in terms of stability and peace."[14]

By 1978 Brzezinski himself was beginning to be "concerned that our human rights policy was in danger of becoming one-sidedly antirightist," and he told President Carter on August 7 that, because of this, the United States was "running the risk of having bad relations simultaneously with Brazil, Chile and Argentina."[15] Exactly how such relations could be repaired without sacrificing high principle, once staked out, stymied Brzezinski as much as anyone,[16] but the loss of military influence and "leverage" was especially distressing to the Defense Department, whose representatives now began to complain publicly about the constrictions of the Humphrey-Kennedy Amendment.[17]

Carter Rethinks

The tentative doubts within the Carter administration over Argentine policy, already nurtured in 1979 by unfortunate events in Nicaragua, exploded into a full-blown controversy in 1980. When the

[12] Miguel S. Wionczek, *Politics and Economics of the External Debt Crisis* (Boulder: Westview Press, 1985), p. 236.

[13] Arms Control and Disarmament Agency, *World Military Expenditures and Arms Transfers, 1967-76* (Washington, D. C., 1978). According to the American League for International Security Assistance, a lobby representing arms manufacturers and three labor unions in the industry, the Argentine provision of the Humphrey-Kennedy Amendment cost the U.S. $813 million in jobs and foreign exchange, "even before a $270 million utilities equipment order was lost by withholding of Eximbank financing." Heliodoro González, "U.S. Arms Transfer Policy in Latin America: Failure of a Policy," *Inter-American Economic Affairs*, XXXII, 2 (1978), p. 79.

[14] Quoted in ibid., p. 85.

[15] Zbigniew Brzezinski, *Power and Principle* (New York: Farrar, Straus and Giroux, 1983), p. 128.

[16] Ibid.

[17] Gonzalez, "U.S. Arms Transfer Policy," p. 85.

Soviet Union invaded Afghanistan in late December 1979, the Carter administration declared an embargo on grain sales to the Soviet Union. This particular response was chosen because, apparently, the president had been assured by his Agriculture Department that "no other country could replace the United States as a major seller to the Soviet Union, a conclusion," Brzezinski archly observed, "that was within days shaken by Argentina's announcement that it would partially replace the American grain shipments."[18]

Quite literally overnight the president discovered an entirely new dimension to U.S.-Argentine relations and, to promote it, he promptly dispatched Lieutenant General Andrew Goodpaster to Buenos Aires. A former commandant of West Point with close ties to the local military establishment, Goodpaster was as persuasive an advocate as Carter might have selected, but the Argentine generals were not moved. It would have been fairly astounding if they had been, however: the service on their foreign debt was beginning to reach serious proportions, and grain sales to the Soviet Union were the country's principal source of hard currency. Not only did Argentina quadruple its sales to the Soviet Union between 1979-1980, but it also reduced customary exports to Italy, Spain, Japan, China, and Peru in order to service Moscow's needs.[19] It is doubtful that this would have occurred in the absence of what the junta regarded as studied provocations by the United States over the previous three and a half years.

Having declared the grain embargo and then failed to make it effective, the president suffered a serious loss of credibility at home and abroad. Worse still, in the process he was forced into the unpleasant role of supplicant before one of the pariah-states he had singled out for exemplary treatment. For his conservative critics, it was a matter of the chickens coming home to roost; for liberals and human rights activists, it was a disturbing sign of potential backsliding, and a blow to the president's credibility with one of his primary constituencies.

Sensing a shift away from what it regarded as high principle, *The New York Times* observed editorially on February 4, 1980:

If reports from Buenos Aires are accurate, Argentina isn't completely deaf to political considerations. It just *might* withhold its grain shipments, if the Carter Administration would drop those complaints of human rights violations in Argentina . . . .

We don't know whether Buenos Aires means that Americans are required to forget the thousands of Argentinians [*sic*] who have vanished completely—or if it will suffice for us just to keep discreetly quiet about the matter. We do know how a transaction of either sort would smell. Let Argentina, if it wishes, pursue a mer-

---

[18] Brzezinski, *Power and Principle*, p. 431.

[19] Testimony of Representative Peter Peyser (Republican of New York) before the Subcommittees on Human Rights and International Organizations and of Inter-American Affairs, House Committee on Foreign Affairs, *Review of United States Policy on Military Assistance to Argentina*, 97th Congress, 1st Sess. (Washington, D.C.: GPO, 1981).

cantilist foreign policy that rewards Soviet aggression. But let not the United States put a price tag on human rights.

The *Times*'s apprehensions were justified. Less than two months later, its own correspondent in Buenos Aires was cabling that:

The Carter Administration has begun a major revision of its policy toward Argentina. This country of 27 million bought $2 billion worth of American goods last year, and is besides a major grain exporter and an emerging nuclear power, with the most advanced technology in Latin America.

The review began when evidence began to accumulate last year that Argentina's military authorities were restraining the worst of the violence by the security forces and bringing the antiguerrilla campaign under centralized control. Fewer than 10 disappearances have been reported since last July.

The United States effort to improve relations quickened after the Soviet Union intervened militarily in Afghanistan . . . .

The failure of General Goodpaster's mission did not discourage Washington from trying to increase commercial sales to Argentina . . . .

The independent Argentine foreign policy is presented by the military regime here as an achievement growing out of Argentina's internal order and economic strength.[20]

It was certainly true, as the reports of Carter's own State Department showed,[21] that the human rights situation in Argentina had improved in the last two years of his administration. The sudden change in Washington's attitude, however, was evidently not inspired by the situation on the ground, but by Argentina's new international relevance and the evident failure of four years of sanctions. This at least was how the impending policy shift was understood by Assistant Secretary of State Patricia Derian, the chief administration official in charge of human rights. As she told a *Times* interviewer on May 30:

Unless things change I'll probably resign in a few days, over a major policy disagreement . . . .

There is about to be a major policy shift on Argentina; a move to normalize our relations and to end our official criticism of the regime . . . .

The decision was taken before [Secretary of State Edmund S.] Muskie came in, but it is probably too late now for them to back down. If they don't I'm leaving, and I won't say it's for "personal reasons."

The interviewer went on to say that

if Patt Derian was identified with any single issue while in office it was her constant, and generally successful battle to distance the United States Government from the military regime in Argentina. That fight now seems to have been lost.[22]

By failing to win re-election in 1980, Carter was liberated from the necessity of reconciling his new foreign-policy realism with the ideological currents represented by Derian and others inside and

[20] Juan de Onís, "Four Years After the Coup," *The New York Times*, March 26, 1980.

[21] See *Country Reports on Human Rights Practices for 1979* and ibid., 1980 (Washington, D.C.: GPO).

[22] Ann Crittenden, "Assistant Secretary of State Patricia M. Derian," *The New York Times*, May 30, 1980.

outside his official family. Thus, what might have become an intra-administration conflict in 1981 could conveniently be pushed over into the more advantageous terrain of partisan politics. And it was.

Argentina Becomes a Domestic Political Issue

The decision of the Carter administration to stigmatize and punish the Argentine government for its human rights violations was not particularly controversial at the time it was taken. Most Americans did not even know where Argentina was, while most of those who did belonged to an elite public with very strong feelings about developments there, virtually all of whom favored a very energetic U.S. response. For example, Argentina was one of the countries targeted by Amnesty International during the mid- and late-seventies for an international letter-writing campaign on behalf of political prisoners; and it received more attention in the editorial pages of *The New York Times* from 1977 to 1980 than any other Latin American country except Chile.

Predictably, there were serious doubts about the Carter policy in the business and banking communities, since Argentina represented one of the largest markets in the region, particularly for expensive technology and military hardware. Leaders of both groups, however, thought it more prudent to express their doubts privately.[1] To all outward appearances, therefore, the Carter policy enjoyed overwhelming public support, such that in 1979 and 1980 Argentina did not figure prominently in any congressional hearing.

Argentina Becomes an Issue

As a distant country where the fundamental interests of the United States were not engaged, Argentina had served as a convenient receptacle for the discharge of the Carter administration's

---

[1] This they did with some vigor. There was considerable private lobbying, particularly by companies like Westinghouse or Allis-Chalmers, which hoped to obtain contracts on a huge hydroelectric project at Yacretá, on the Paraguayan border. In 1978, the Export-Import Bank, on instructions from the White House, refused to lend Argentina $280 million to buy electric generators from Allis-Chalmers; by the time the decision was reversed, under heavy lobbying from American companies active in Latin America, the contract had gone elsewhere. This was when the human rights policy was at its height. Later, when Carter was reversing himself, Undersecretary of Commerce Luther H. Hodges, Jr., was dispatched to Buenos Aires, as *The New York Times* reported on March 26, 1980, "to assure the Argentine authorities that the United States Export-Import Bank would provide $700 million to finance construction of a big hydroelectric dam on the Paraná River and supply turbines and generators if United States companies were given the contract."

moral indignation over the state of human rights in many other countries. Argentina's utility in this regard survived into the Reagan years, becoming equally useful as a battering ram for the liberal left to discredit the new president's foreign policies, particularly his preference for persuasion and quiet diplomacy when dealing with authoritarian allies, and his conviction that there was a qualitative difference between dictatorships of the left and the right.

In the early weeks of the new administration, *The Washington Post* had expressed the hope that the human rights debate might be rescued "from the abstractions and rigidities of the political trench warfare that has come to substitute for reasoned argument in recent years." Turning to the specific case of Argentina, it pointed out that "when you do look more closely . . . you see a place that fits neither side of the old debate."[2] Perhaps so, but this did not prevent political trench warfare from erupting anew, often with the same participants lobbing the same explosives against one another. The only difference was the change in positions; yesterday's opposition now bore the responsibility for policy outcomes, while yesterday's government could now indulge uninhibitedly in lurid accusations.

The opening salvo was a statement by the new secretary of state, Alexander M. Haig, Jr., at his first press conference on January 28, 1981.

International terrorism will take the place of human rights . . . because it is the ultimate abuse of human rights. And it's time that it be addressed with greater clarity and greater effectiveness by Western nations and the United States as well.[3]

While Haig insisted that "human rights is an essential and fundamental aspect of American foreign policy," he added that

when you remove it from the mainstream of fundamental policymaking and give it an extraordinary role in organizational terms, you frequently result in distortions [*sic*] that probably put in jeopardy the well-meaning objective you seek to achieve. So I would like to see some organizational changes in the period ahead—no deemphasis, a change in priorities.[4]

From these almost incoherent remarks, garbled further by journalistic translation, the military in Argentina (as well as in Chile, Uruguay, Guatemala, and Haiti) imagined that their problems with the United States were over. After all, they reasoned, what, if not terrorism aided and abetted by the Soviet Union, had they been fighting all these years? To discourage such a crude reading of Washington's intentions would probably have required very energetic denials, amounting to nothing less than a reaffirmation of the very policies Reagan had just successfuly campaigned against. In Buenos Aires, the euphoria in official circles was further enhanced by hand-

---

[2] "What About Argentina?" *The Washington Post*, March 21, 1981.
[3] *Department of State Bulletin* (Special), February 1981, p. J.
[4] Ibid.

wringing comments by the prestige press, liberal Democrats in Congress, and the human rights community, all anxious for reasons of their own to put the darkest possible construction on Haig's remarks.

Utterly forgotten were the questions raised by the experience of Carter's last year in office. How useful were sanctions beyond a certain point? How much was Argentina's friendship worth? Was conciliation a better instrument for improved leverage than continued ostracism? Was a change of policy worth a try? In the best of times these problems would have been difficult to resolve, but given the new partisan environment in which they were being debated, as well as the emotional charge of the human rights issue itself, they were particularly nettlesome.

They were also probably not worth the political cost that the Reagan administration had to pay, either. Clearly, some change in policy was called for, since to continue Carter's earlier policy of confrontation virtually assured that bilateral relations would never move off-center, where they had become mired in 1979 and 1980. However, to appear excessively conciliatory to the authorities in Buenos Aires—unless rather spectacular results could be accomplished in the very short term—left one open to charges of condoning human rights violations and, what was worse, attempting to consolidate and perpetuate the military regime that had committed them.

It was difficult for the new administration to avoid the latter trap, since like its predecessor it came to Washington determined to remake the world. While some of the charges made against it were grossly unfair, unquestionably the Reagan team shared a strongly counter-revisionist view of American foreign policy reminiscent of the 1950s, when friends and enemies were easier to identify, moral choices much simpler, and the domestic political environment less contentious and complex. It also represented a reaction to the spirit of national self-denigration evident in the subtext of much of Carter's rhetoric, and an egregious "double standard" in human rights policy,[5] whose existence most liberals denied but also defended.[6]

Since the Carter State Department had eventually concluded on its own that the human rights situation in Argentina had perceptibly improved, presumably a new look at policy instruments was in order. So much for theory. In practice, Argentina offered critics of the administration, who had been recently defeated in a humiliating electoral contest, a golden opportunity to put the Reagan team on the defensive. It could not have come at a more opportune moment,

---

[5] The definitive indictment is, of course, the now famous article by Jeane J. Kirkpatrick, "Dictatorships and Double Standards," *Commentary*, November 1979.

[6] In most cases this was not because they sympathized in any way with communist regimes, but rather were possessed of an almost evangelical desire to prove the United States morally superior. I exclude professional "human rights activists," who in many cases clearly were (and are) supporters of the revolutionary left in Third World countries.

because Carter himself had been on the defensive throughout 1980. Events in Iran and Nicaragua had raised serious questions about the utility of the human rights issue as an instrument for effective social change. Even in El Salvador, where military assistance had been suspended in 1977, the administration in its final days found it necessary to resume ties with the armed forces, faced there with a "final offensive" by the FDR-FMLN guerrilla army.

The first engagement between recent victors and vanquished occurred over Ernest Lefever, nominated by President Reagan to replace Patricia Derian as assistant secretary of state for human rights and humanitarian affairs. Lefever immediately became the target of an unprecedented campaign by church and human rights lobbies. To deliver the knockout blow against Reagan's nominee, they brought to Washington Argentine newspaper publisher Jacobo Timerman, whose chronicle of physical and psychological mistreatment in the junta's jaws had just been published.[7] Though Timerman—widely regarded in Argentina, if not in the United States, as a charlatan[8]— had never met Lefever and knew little or nothing about him, he assured a dinner meeting at the Carnegie Endowment in Washington, "if Lefever is defeated, it will mean that Americans are not going back to the era of the cold war and McCarthy."[9] Within days Lefever was forced to withdraw from the confirmation process.

At the same time, the administration exposed its flank to critics by rushing forward to embrace the junta in Buenos Aires before it had much to show for its troubles. In March President-designate[10] Roberto Viola was received at the White House as the United States revealed it was considering lifting the embargo on military aid; a few days before, the administration had formally requested $50,000 in military training grants for Argentina (with an equal amount for Chile).[11] *The Washington Post* accepted the administration's logic that "Argentina is not the same place it was when Jimmy Carter entered the White House," and as such "a different sort of human rights policy" might be in order. It even conceded that Viola represented "the forces of cautious, controlled relaxation: the only kind of change feasible in Argentina."[12]

---

[7] Jacobo Timerman, *Prisoner without a Name, Cell without a Number* (New York: Alfred A. Knopf, 1981).

[8] See my article, "The Timerman Case," *Commentary*, July 1981. Though his account of his experiences in Argentine jails seems accurate enough, Timerman was less than candid about the causes of his arrest and the real nature of his relationship with the junta. He also misrepresented the situation of the Jewish community in Argentina, and its treatment by the military.

[9] *The New York Times*, May 20, 1981. For Lefever's activities behind the scenes in his nomination, see *The Washington Post*, May 20, 1981.

[10] Technically "President-elect," though "elected" only by a parliament of generals and admirals, for a four-year term.

[11] *The New York Times*, March 1, 1988; and ibid., March 13, 1988.

[12] "What About Argentina?" *The New York Times*, March 21, 1988.

But *The New York Times* came closer to reflecting the views of the liberal community and the Democratic party, which preferred to use the new administration's Argentine policy as the litmus test of its fundamental decency. While the *Times* did not attribute all unpleasant events in and near Buenos Aires to the White House, it steadfastly refused to accept the notion that any improvements could be related to efforts at "quiet diplomacy." For example, commenting editorially on the recent release of several human rights activists, it expressed total certainty that this was not a response to Reagan policy, which it described as "withholding public criticism of such a brazen crackdown." Rather, it opined, "the evidence suggests quite the reverse: Argentines responded to vehement world-wide protest," including warnings by Senator Daniel Patrick Moynihan that such events would undermine the upcoming visit of President-elect Viola.[13] Pulling all the rhetorical stops, the *Times* featured columnist Anthony Lewis:

Are things at such a point that we Americans must embrace torturers and murderers as our allies, and proclaim their values, their God, as ours?

Can we conceivably believe that embracing them as our own will strengthen our influence in this hemisphere? . . . What kind of country are we?[14]

Congress Takes a Hand

Lefever's nomination was one thing, an innocuous "private visit" by the military president-designate of Argentina yet another. But the new administration's request to lift several existing sanctions against Argentina—not merely military aid and training, but also programmed opposition at the multilateral lending institutions and the Export-Import Bank—provoked a flurry of activity on Capitol Hill. When it did, the Argentine story entered a new phase.

In April, a joint hearing of the Subcommittees on Human Rights and International Organizations and Inter-American Affairs of the House Foreign Affairs Committee was convoked to consider the administration's recommendation to repeal the embargo on arms sales and military training (the Humphrey-Kennedy Amendment). Another was convened in July by the Subcommittee on International Development Institutions and Finance of the House Committee on Banking, Finance, and Urban Affairs, to examine Reagan's decision to cease opposition to multilateral bank loans for Argentina, Chile, Paraguay, and Uruguay on human rights grounds.

The April hearing on military assistance gave considerable symbolic importance to the impending repeal of Humphrey-Kennedy; Representative Michael Barnes (Democrat of Maryland) declared in his opening statement that he was "deeply concerned that the lifting of this sanction may be seen as a change in our attitude towards terrorism and torture."[15] Representative Don Bonker (Democrat of Washington) went even further, noting that the administration's proposal was all of a piece with other attempts to "reverse U. S. foreign policy," including restrictions on covert activities in Africa and elsewhere,[16] as if that alone made the request unworthy of serious consideration.

Almost from the very beginning, the hearing veered away from an objective consideration of the human rights situation in Argentina to a discussion of the morality and convenience of the proposed new policy. The entire session divided not over whether things had recently taken a turn for the better in Argentina, but whether it was appropriate to take concrete notice of the fact and whether, too, further improvement could be expected by lifting (as opposed to retaining) the arms embargo. (Nobody seemed to think it possible that the embargo might be irrelevant one way or the other.)

Two administration witnesses, former congressman James E. Karth (a registered foreign agent of the Argentine government), and James D. Theberge (a prominent economic consultant with diplomatic experience) tried to focus the members' attention on pragmatic considerations: the situation on the ground, the ineffectiveness of the embargo, the evolving human rights environment, the counterproductive nature of U.S. sanctions, the loss of jobs and foreign sales to other suppliers, the Argentine response to the grain embargo, and the need to give the administration the means to respond more flexibly to situations overseas.[17] They convinced few, and some members of the subcommittee seemed irritated by the intrusion of facts into what they took to be a more rarified debate.

Witnesses opposed to the repeal made up a *who's who* of the human rights lobby: Patricia Feeney of Amnesty International, Orville Schell of the Lawyers' Committee on Human Rights in New York, and Reverend Joseph Eldridge of the Washington Office on Latin America. They emphasized the continuing problem of disappearances and the persistence of persons being held without trial, as well as the government's continued refusal to account for missing persons. For his part, Eldridge insisted that "almost every major improvement in the human rights situation can be traced to some form of international pressure."[18]

By suddenly focusing on accountability for past events, as opposed to the evolving situation within Argentina, the human rights community virtually guaranteed that there could be never sufficient

---

[15] *Review of United States Policy on Military Assistance to Argentina*, 97th Congress, 1st Sess. (Washington, D.C.: GPO, 1981), p. 1.
[16] Ibid., p. 2.
[17] Ibid., pp. 17-47.
[18] Ibid., pp. 64-126; Eldridge on p. 118.

"improvement" to merit serious response by the United States, short of a radical change in regime. Schell himself, by far the most honest and objective of the three witnesses, admitted that this was asking for something (then president-elect) General Roberto Viola probably could not do. "He is controlled by the military . . . . It is very difficult, very difficult."[19]

Representative Dan Mica (Democrat of Florida) struck an uncommonly pragmatic note: he conceded that the issue was falling prey to partisan politics, wished it were otherwise, but confessed himself unsure which way to go.[20] Representative Milicent Fenwick (Republican of New Jersey) conceded that the embargo "puts us in great difficulty when we have absolutely essential security interests in certain parts of the world." But, she added, "for the time being, and given that we do not want to give the wrong symbol, it might be wiser not to simply wipe out this prohibition."

When she asked Ambassador Theberge for his judgment, he replied, "We are far more effective in achieving our objectives when we create the basis for closer relations with other countries," re-emphasizing the primacy of domestic political factors within Argentina, as opposed to foreign pressures.[21] He stressed again that events within Argentina were taking care of themselves, and that the generalized trend was bound to continue. But to this Representative Bonker responded, "I do not think improvement, per se, is sufficient reason, because it could improve from worse to bad." Taking his cue from Schell, he concluded that if the Argentine government wanted to offer "an expression of good faith in order to warrant more positive action here in Congress, then they ought to be forthcoming with some of the names of the disappeared . . . [or] it could release many of these political prisoners."[22]

The second hearing was prompted by a letter from the Treasury Department to the appropriate congressional authorities informing them that the current human rights situation in Argentina (as well as in Chile, Paraguay, and Uruguay) no longer required U.S. opposition to multilateral development bank loans. Members were indignant that the correspondence had been dispatched on July 1, 1981, while Congress was in recess, and also that, by failing to consult with either the chairman or ranking member of the Subcommittee on International Development Institutions and Finance, the administration was technically in violation of existing legislation.[23] Congressional feathers were ruffled, but not so much that an objective assessment could not be made.

[19] Ibid., pp. 127-28.
[20] Ibid., p. 52.
[21] Ibid., p. 57.
[22] Ibid., p. 62.
[23] PL 95-118 (1977), Title VII of the International Financial Institutions Act.

The question of multilateral lending could be approached more dispassionately because the legislative history of PL 95-118 (1977) was very different from that of the Humphrey-Kennedy Amendment. The Carter administration itself had originally opposed legislated U.S. votes at the multilateral banks because, in its view, it introduced excessive rigidity into the diplomatic-financial process. The pertinent amendment, sponsored by Representative Tom Harkin (Democrat of Iowa) had actually been defeated in subcommittee vote, only to pass on the full house floor.[24] As Representative John J. LaFalce (Democrat of New York) remarked quite rightly, he did not see "that great a difference at all with respect to the desire of this administration and the Carter Administration" on the question of flexibility.[25]

The differences turned instead on whether the subcommittee agreed with the administration that the situation in Argentina merited a more favorable U.S. response to that country's loan applications. As the chief administration witness, Ernest B. Johnson, Jr.,[26] reminded the members, the Carter administration itself had altered its voting policies toward Argentina in its final months "to recognize the improvements that have occurred."[27]

In subsequent testimony, there was less division within the committee than between its members and the opposition witnesses. There was much haggling across the table over what a "consistent pattern" of gross human rights violations might be, and also over whether there had been any improvement in Argentina at all. Hurst Hannum of Amnesty International, whose characterizations seemed a bit extreme for some members, was forced to back off. "Certainly," he conceded, "there has been a lessening of the number of disappearances. If I said something to the contrary, I did not mean that." But, he added quite revealingly, "When I said there was no substantial change, I meant that there had been no substantial change in the institutional structures that permitted the disappearances to continue."[28] In other words, nothing less than a change of regime would qualify as an improvement, and therefore merit even an incrementally positive U.S. response.

The Reagan administration finally compromised on military aid by allowing the Humphrey-Kennedy Amendment to be replaced by another law, Section 725 of the International Security and Development Cooperation Act (1980), which permitted the sale of arms

---

[24] *Human Rights and U.S. Policy in the Multilateral Development Banks*, Hearings before the Subcommittee on International Development Institutions and Finance of the Committee on Banking, Finance and Urban Affairs, House of Representatives, 97th Congress, 1st Sess. (Washington, D.C.: GPO, 1981), p. 22.

[25] Ibid., p. 24.

[26] Johnson was senior deputy assistant secretary of state, Bureau of Economic and Business Affairs, Department of State.

[27] *Human Rights and U. S. Policy in the Multilateral Development Banks*, p. 47.

[28] Ibid., p. 338.

and the resumption of military training for both Argentina and Chile when and if the president of the United States certified that a significant (though unverified) improvement in human rights had occurred.

On balance, the Argentine issue resulted in a net loss for the new administration. The evident domestic political costs made certification a virtual impossibility.[29] But merely by proposing to sell arms to Argentina, the Reagan team allowed the opposition to attack it from the moral high ground, obscuring the fact that the Carter administration itself had rarely been of one mind on the relationship between fact and policy—much less that it had also opposed excessive legislative restraints on some diplomatic instruments. All of the finer points of the debate were lost: the only thing most people who read newspapers or watched television were likely to learn was that Reagan wanted to give money and arms to Argentine torturers and murderers, and that was that. No doubt the junta in Buenos Aires appreciated the gesture, but whether its friendship was worth such extravagance remained to be seen.

[29] It came only after the fall of the military junta and the inauguration of an elected president (Raúl Alfonsín) in early 1984.

An Argentine-American Alliance, 1981-1982

Where Was Argentina Heading, 1980-1982?

In the *Commentary* essay that first brought her to the attention of President Reagan,[1] Jeane J. Kirkpatrick discussed the morphology of democracy and dictatorship, and the relationship between regime types and the prospects for political change. Her theoretical apparatus was not new: in fact, most of the concepts she employed were part of the broader patrimony of American social science derived from classics published in the 1940s and 1950s: Hannah Arendt's *The Origins of Totalitarianism*, Siegfried Neumann's *Totalitarian Dictatorship and Autocracy*, and Seymour Martin Lipset's *Political Man*. Adumbrated versions of these arguments circulated in the literature throughout the 1950s and 1960s as well,[2] and only the power of the Vietnam trauma could have been so amnesic in its effect as to make Kirkpatrick's categories seem novel. But what made the article (and its author) a *cause célèbre* was the fact that for the first time these commonly accepted categories of analysis were applied to a concrete foreign-policy problem in ways that the liberal community found ideologically and emotionally distasteful.

What Kirkpatrick did in "Dictatorships and Double Standards" was to examine critically two cases—Nicaragua and Iran—in which the United States purposefully undermined friendly authoritarian regimes only to pave the way for communism in the first instance, radical Islam in the second. Her analysis was careful and complex; she did not "favor" friendly tyrannies as such, nor suggest that any social or political change in the Third World automatically led to a deterioration of political freedom or the interests of the United States. What she *did* say was that not all countries were ready for democracy; that some kinds of dictatorships (authoritarian) were less noxious and permanent than others (totalitarian); and that the United States

[1] "Dictatorships and Double Standards," *Commentary*, November 1979.
[2] See, for example, Samuel Huntington, *Political Order in Changing Societies* (New Haven: Yale University Press, 1968), widely used as text.

should not automatically regard all so-called progressive forces for change as necessarily positive.

There was no instance, she wrote, of "revolutionary 'socialist' or Communist society being democratized," but right-wing autocracies "do sometimes evolve into democracies—given time, propitious economic, social, and political circumstances, talented leaders, and a strong indigenous demand for representative governments." Something of the kind, she added, writing in 1979 "is in progress on the Iberian peninsula, and the first steps have been taken in Brazil." The function of foreign policy under such circumstances, she wrote, was "to understand the process of change, and then, like Marxists, to align ourselves with history, hoping to contribute a bit of stability along the way."

Since traditional autocracies did permit limited participation, "it is not impossible that U.S. policy could effectively encourage this process of liberalization and democratization, provided that the effort is not made at a time when the incumbent government is fighting for its life against violent adversaries," and also that the "proposed reforms are aimed at producing gradual change rather than perfect democracy overnight." To accomplish this, she said, policy makers needed "to understand how actual democracies have come into being. History is a better guide than good intentions."

How applicable was this framework to Argentina in 1981-82? While the country had never demonstrated a great affinity for democracy, there were at least abundant historical precedents for gradual devolution from military to civilian rule—in 1932, 1946, 1958, 1963, and 1973. On each occasion, a military government which had come to power through a *coup d'état* had called elections, even though in two instances, 1958 and 1973, the victory of a candidate unacceptable to the armed forces was a virtual certainty.

Beyond that, there had been an unquestionable improvement in the human rights situation, apparent not only in statistics but in the texture of daily life. As Ambassador Theberge had pointed out in the April hearings on military assistance, the number of persons detained by the Executive Power (the so-called PEN prisoners)[3] had dropped to 900, or approximately 10 percent of what it had been in 1974.[4] The annual number of "disappearances" had dropped below two digits. The curfew had been lifted, the harsher aspects of press censorship were abolished, and visitors to the country in 1980 noted an atmosphere of relative normality.

[3] PEN = Poder Ejecutivo Nacional, or National Executive Power. As is the case in most Latin American countries, there is no right of *habeas corpus* in Argentina, and persons can be incarcerated on executive order for an indeterminate period.

[4] *Review of United States Policy on Military Assistance to Argentina*, p. 47.

There was also a cautious shift in the nature of the military government itself. President Viola, inaugurated in March 1981, had dramatically increased the participation of civilians: only seven of the governors named to Argentina's twenty-two provinces were men in uniform, and the key cabinet ministers were now civilians as well. Most outstanding of these was the new foreign minister, Oscar Camilión, a lawyer and academic close to former president Arturo Frondizi. The same month it took office, the Viola administration permitted four unions to hold elections for the first time since 1976. And the Interior Ministry announced that political activities would legally resume sometime in the course of 1981 or early 1982.[5] The minister himself engaged in a first round of discussions with opposition party and labor leaders in June 1981, and a second one in August.

At the same time, however, some signs pointed in the opposite direction. A new law, supposedly in the making, governing political parties was continually delayed, and in fact had not been published at the time war broke out with Great Britain in April 1982. Nor was it clear that Viola would be the last of Argentina's military presidents. When asked by a Greek journalist whether free elections would be established after his term, outgoing president General Jorge Videla remarked rather delphically that "prerequisites do not yet exist . . . . If they exist after three years . . . the answer will be affirmative." But, he remarked, "if elections are not held there may possibly be a transitional period, for example, a referendum." And, he added in passing, "during the dialogue which the government has begun, none of the political leaders who has been asked has demanded urgent elections of any kind."[6]

More disturbing still were remarks by General Leopoldo Galtieri, commander in chief of the army and senior member of the junta, who told cadets at the El Palomar Military College in late May that while many were asking the military to accelerate the transfer of power, it could only take place "when the conditions are right." Other military "processes" over the last fifty years had "lost their bearing, and it was thought that there was an electoral solution to political problems." The history of successive failures suggested the need "not to commit a similar error this time."[7] For his part, President Viola stated flatly that "it is impossible to fix a set date for the return to democracy . . . . Elections in themselves are not the purpose of democracy . . . . I have not been designated president to liquidate the national reorganization process."[8]

[5] FBIS—*LAT*, April 8, 1981.
[6] Ibid., January 2, 1981.
[7] Ibid., June 2, 1981.
[8] Ibid., September 18, 1981.

The more positive signs pointed to a traditional Argentine solution, that is, the gradual transfer of power to civilians, culminating in elections, precisely as had occurred in 1958, 1963, and, most recently, in 1973. Probably much of the political class expected this as well, since most of its activities were intended to accelerate that eventual date. For example, the Buenos Aires branch of the Radical party, the country's second largest, criticized the government's economic performance and called for a change in political course, but added that it "wants this process to succeed . . . as long as it arrives at returning to institutional normality and a constitutional regime."[9] Similar sentiments were issued at about the same time by Conservative and Peronist politicians.[10]

A second possibility was some form of *continuismo*, through the creation of an official party, the unrealized dream of every military government in Argentina since 1930. Thus, navy commander Admiral Armando Lambruschini told the press in December 1980 that "the Navy would like to see the appearance of renewal political parties or new currents of opinion,"[11] and several Conservative politicians were suddenly declared "presidential advisers."[12]

A third was some form of understanding (*concertación*) between the right wing of Peronism and the armed forces, an arrangement Radical leader Raúl Alfonsín later denounced as a "military-syndicalist pact."[13] Such, of course, was the genesis of the first Perón government (1946-1952), an unbeatable political combination whose obvious possibilities continued to haunt both officers and labor leaders, particularly after the great man's death in 1974 with no obvious successor in sight. Of all the opposition leaders, the Peronist party's first vice president Felipe Deolindo Bittel was the most consistently obsequious in his remarks about the military government, this despite the fact that until the last days of 1980, his titular leader, former president Isabel Perón, was under house arrest. Peronist leaders were meeting secretly with government officials and military men more or less continuously throughout 1981, and with President Galtieri himself publicly in early 1982, although Bittel was insisting to the press that these deliberations were strictly "unofficial."[14]

Fourth and finally, there was the possibility of a "neo-Peronist" solution in the person of retired Admiral Eduardo Massera, who until 1980 had been the navy member of the ruling junta. A bluff, handsome sailor with considerable personal charm, Massera was also one

---

[9] Ibid., April 24, 1981.

[10] Ibid., April 30, 1981.

[11] *Clarín* (Buenos Aires), December 31, 1980.

[12] FBIS—*LAT*, May 8, 1981.

[13] This was in part inspired by the fact that the unions—the chief prop of Isabel Perón within the party—had no more interest than the military in a serious examination of human rights offenses during the 1974-76 period.

[14] FBIS—*LAT*, March 15, 27, 1982.

of the most cynical practitioners of a politics of expediency. No sooner had he retired from the service than he suddenly began to publicly criticize his former colleagues, particularly with regard to economic policy (a favored target was its expressed intention to privatize large segments of the public sector). By early 1982, however, he was even beginning to toy with the issue of the "disappeared."[15]

In July 1981, Massera had assembled a coalition of Peronist and Conservative political figures, businessmen, and union leaders, "under the spiritual leadership," as he put it, of Vice-Admiral (retired) Eduardo Fracassi and Alfredo Vezza, editor in chief of a new biweekly magazine, *Cambio*, founded to advance Massera's political fortunes.[16]

An Argentine daily with close ties to the navy, *Convicción*, likewise began to exhibit *masserista* political tendencies. In August, as the admiral was on a semi-official visit to Romania, his friends launched his new political vehicle which, with characteristic Argentine drollery, they called the Social Democratic party.

Outside observers would have been pressed to say which of these various outcomes was the most likely. The Reagan administration proceeded as if things would sort themselves out in Argentina much as they had in the past—that sooner or later the military would tire of political responsibility and call elections; in the meanwhile, relations could continue as usual or perhaps a bit better than usual. This sanguine view overlooked certain qualitative differences between the military government of 1976-1982 and all those that had preceded it.[17] Given the sheer number of people liquidated in the "dirty war" against subversion, far-reaching moral and juridical issues would eventually have to be confronted. Under such circumstances, whatever good sense might otherwise counsel, it was unlikely that *this* time the armed forces would risk turning authority back to civilians except under very special conditions.

Such conditions would have had to include some kind of arrangement with the politicians not to look too closely into recent events or to assign responsibility for them, an agenda subsumed by the curious Argentine word *concertación*. Such an agreement was being fitfully sought throughout 1981-82, but with no real enthusiasm and certainly no sense of urgency. The military preferred to bide its time until the politicians freely offered them such a deal, which is why all of the other characteristic features of Argentine political

[15] At first he seemed to call for an accounting, but when pressured for clarification, he backtracked and merely stated that he favored publication of complete lists of "casualties on both sides." Ibid., January 26, 1982.

[16] Ibid., July 7, 1981.

[17] It also overlooked the fact that "constitutionalist" or "constitutionalist"-leaning officers had been fairly well purged from the armed forces after a coup in 1966. Thus even General Viola was once part of a "hard-line faction" of young officers; by 1981 they were generals and admirals.

devolution (legalization of political activity, a parties' statute, and so forth) were continually postponed.

The national mood, however, did not suggest many alternatives to working with the existing regime in Argentina and hoping for the best. Even Orville Schell admitted at the April hearings in Washington that there was no pressing concern within Argentina for the kinds of things that were dividing congressional and administration forces in the United States. Asked to describe the views of the "man in the street there," he replied, "I would have to say with some dismay that I found very, very little interest . . . in the subject of human rights and the kinds of things that are actually written in the Argentine constitution. It is kind of discouraging."[18] The *Buenos Aires Herald*, a highly respected independent English-language daily second to none in its criticism of the military government, went even further, declaring editorially that "bad as the 'process' [the dictatorship's name for itself] has been politically, economically, socially, and ethically, there is no reason to think that if it came to the abrupt end many would prefer, it would be replaced by something obviously better. On the contrary . . . its successor would almost certainly be a good deal worse."[19] Such was the environment in which the peculiar Argentine-American alliance of 1981-82 was forged.

"At an Optimal Level": Bilateral Relations, 1981-1982

The change in U.S. administrations in 1981 had important consequences for the bilateral relationship. As noted above, the Reagan team was prepared to do business with its Argentine counterpart, whereas its predecessor had striven to keep it at arm's length. To some extent, however, Argentina was merely an incidental beneficiary of the counter-revisionist mood engulfing Washington at the time (as were South Africa, South Korea, and Chile). However, in one area—Central America—the two governments were already pursuing explicitly congruent policies and objectives.

Even before the advent of the Reagan administration, the Argentine military had been actively involved in Central America. During the Nicaraguan civil war (1977-78), Argentina had provided that country's dynastic ruler, Anastasio Somoza Debayle, with weapons and technical military assistance after the United States had abandoned him, imposed an arms embargo, and pressured its allies (particularly Israel) to follow suit. Argentina was also active in El Salvador, assisting the military junta (and then its successor, the civilian-military junta that took over in July 1979), against Cuban-backed guerrilla forces.

[18] *Review of United States Policy on Military Assistance*, p. 127.
[19] James Neilsen, "Dangerous Perspectives," February 4, 1982, reproduced in FBIS—*LAT*, February 9, 1982.

Central America was, to say the least, a highly novel area of Argentine foreign-policy concern. For the military government, however, special ideological and personal reasons encouraged a presence there. Many of the Argentine terrorists who survived the "dirty war" at home subsequently escaped to Central America and settled there, some becoming actively involved in the Sandinista army or the Salvadoran guerrilla movement. These exiles were seen by the Argentine military as part of a worldwide conspiracy to bring down Latin American military institutions and Western civilization with it. The reluctance of the Carter administration to see matters in quite the same light merely redoubled the conviction of the Argentine military that—the United States having ceded the field of battle to the Communists—there was an overarching need for an alternative source of military and political assistance within the region.

Little is known about the precise dimensions of the Argentine military presence in El Salvador, but it is reasonable to assume that it increased considerably after the Reagan administration defined the country as being of central concern in January 1981. Unusually large Argentine military missions were present throughout the region[20] and, as is now known, Argentine officers played a central role in organizing the first armed resistance to the Sandinista government in Nicaragua, working out of Miami with former officers of the National Guard. Theoretically these things could have happened apart from any specific U.S.-Argentine understanding, but too many large fragments of evidence have surfaced to believe that there was none.[21]

The Argentines were particularly useful to the Reagan administration at this particular juncture because, during most of 1981, the latter was engaged in a pitched battle with Congress over military aid to El Salvador. Though the legislative branch never "pulled the plug" on the fragile military-civilian junta there, it threatened continually to do so. Thus Argentina (along with Israel, Taiwan, South Africa, and possibly South Korea) became fallback sources of military aid in the event of a congressionally mandated cut-off.

Argentina was also of modest use to the Reagan administration as one Latin American "major" that unambiguously backed U.S. Central American policy at the Organization of American States, the United Nations, and other forums, precisely at a time when that policy was being attacked frontally by Mexico, and while democratic allies like Colombia or Venezuela either dithered or refused to define themselves. Precisely what the Argentines were promised in exchange for their assistance has never been made clear; it may well

[20] According to U.S. Embassy sources in November 1981, there were no fewer than 150 officers and men stationed in Honduras.

[21] See Shirley Christian, *Nicaragua: Revolution in the Family* (New York: Random House, 1985), pp. 193-292; *The New York Times*, March 3, 1982; and less reliably, Bob Woodward, *Veil* (New York: Simon and Schuster, 1987), especially pp. 172-77.

have been that Washington assumed that since their Central American policy had a logic of its own, there was no need to offer a specific quid pro quo.

The United States did, however, end Argentina's isolation, largely through symbolic gestures, the significance of which should not be underestimated from the junta's point of view. As noted, the new administration made a costly attempt to lift the arms embargo; reversed U.S. voting policies at the multilateral development banks; and received General Viola with honors due a genuine president-elect in March 1981. It also dispatched U.S. Ambassador to the United Nations Jeane Kirkpatrick to Buenos Aires the following August, and received army commander General Leopoldo Galtieri in Washington in October. In March 1982, with Assistant Secretary of State for Inter-American Affairs Thomas Enders about to arrive for a major visit, Argentina's ambassador in Washington, Esteban Takacs, noted that the bilateral relationship was now "at an optimal level."[22]

Apart from Central America, however, there were strict limits to the new U.S.-Argentine entente. Although the military made much of its identification with the values of what it liked to call "Western Christian civilization," Foreign Minister Camilión declared in April 1981 that Argentina would remain "independent of the two blocs" and continue to be active in the Non-Aligned Movement.[23] Economic relations with the Eastern bloc continued without interruption,[24] and the Argentine government even authorized the sale of 300 trucks and spare parts to Cuba from Ford's Argentine subsidiary[25]—this in clear contravention of the spirit, if not precisely the letter, of U.S. policy.

The Viola government also firmly refused the entreaties of the Reagan administration to provide troops for the Sinai Peace Force, which it was assembling to implement the Camp David Accords. And when in early 1981 the State Department made some cautious remarks "encouraging" the Argentine authorities to disclose whatever they knew of the fate of disappeared persons to their families, Nicanor Costa Méndez, who replaced Camilión as foreign minister in December 1981, frostily replied: "We do not need anyone to encourage us on this subject, and I would say that when someone tries to encourage us, they discourage us."[26]

Moreover, even in its very limited form, the Argentine-American alliance carried high domestic political costs in both countries. The fact that a military dictatorship with a bloody record of its own was

[22] FBIS—*LAT*, March 2, 1982.
[23] Ibid., April 24, 1981.
[24] It was reported, in February 1981, that there were "no plans" to reduce grain sales to the Soviet Union and reallocate those quotas to Brazil and Iraq, though by this time President Reagan had already promised to lift the U.S. embargo. Ibid., February 16, 1981.
[25] Ibid., October 16, 1981.
[26] Ibid, March 24, 1982.

perceived (or represented itself) to be the chief prop of the Reagan administration's Central American policy was not a persuasive argument on its behalf within the intellectual and media community or in Congress. And in Argentina itself, the presence of military advisers in El Salvador and elsewhere in Central America—though steadfastly denied by the government[27]—aroused traditional sentiments of isolationism, anti-Americanism, and nationalism, which the opposition was quick to exploit.

No doubt the Argentine government *thought*, or occasionally pretended to think, that the convergence of U.S. and Argentine goals in Central America and the evident cordiality of senior Reagan administration officials meant a wholly new, better period in bilateral relations. As President-designate Viola effused in Washington at the end of his visit to the United States, "I have encountered an understanding that exceeded my most exaggerated hopes."[28] Retiring Argentine ambassador in Washington Jorge A. Aja Espil assured his countrymen that "Reagan is a friend of Argentina and of President Viola, and this sets a course toward future possibilities."[29] Camilión, after meeting for six hours with Ambassador Kirkpatrick, said that "the United States government has made a decision to make progress in its relations with Argentina in the most harmonious way possible."[30] Former foreign minister Raúl Quijano, who accompanied General Galtieri to Washington, told newsmen that U.S. officials on that occasion had given the army chief "exceptional treatment . . . the U.S. government obviously tried to make him feel at ease, and show him the friendship which exists between the two countries."[31] Quite apart from a traditional Argentine penchant to exaggerate the country's international importance, these remarks were meant as much as anything else for domestic consumption—to exaggerate the degree of foreign support for the regime, convince its doubting or vacillating supporters, and demoralize its opponents. Still, the Argentines probably believed most of what they were hearing. Within weeks of Galtieri's visit, however, the fragility of the Argentine-American alliance became painfully evident.

The Slippery Path to Decline, November 1981-April 1982

Even before President Viola assumed office, it was obvious that Argentina was gradually but unavoidably approaching a major economic crisis. By the end of 1979, the foreign debt had reached $20 billion, more than double what it had been in 1966. The following

---

[27] Ibid., March 22, 1982, among many others. The official position of the Argentine government was that it would give the government of El Salvador economic and military assistance if it was requested. It denied, however, any active involvement by Argentine soldiers.

[28] Ibid., March 19, 1981.

[29] Ibid., June 16, 1981.

[30] Ibid., August 6, 1981.

[31] Ibid., November 19, 1981.

year, government and business deficits approached $4 billion, which encouraged a new cycle of foreign borrowing. In February 1981, the government declared a 9 percent devaluation of the peso, creating a panic in financial circles and leading thousands to line up at banks and exchange shops to buy dollars. In April, the financial system was shaken anew by the government's liquidation of the largest private bank in Argentina, apparently because its owner was known to have close ties to Admiral Massera. This in turn led to the collapse of the secondary financial market and the demise of two other private banks. The Central Bank was compelled to disburse $2 billion more to shore up the private banking system.

The appointment of conservative banker Roberto Alemann to be economic minister in December led to new austerity policies aimed at reducing the deficit, but without notable impact on business confidence. At the same time, Alemann's policies provoked heated dissent for, among other things, he proposed to sell off government-owned utilities and other companies. This inevitably implied a decline in public employment, where one and possibly two out of every three middle-class Argentines found their professional niche.[32] More to the point, the new finance minister's plan was highly unpopular with the military, since publicly owned industries typically provided well-paying berths for retired officers. A few days after Alemann announced his plan, former president (1966-1970) General Juan Carlos Onganía threw down the gauntlet, declaring to an audience in La Plata that "the era of economic liberalism is coming to an end . . . . The coming battle [in Argentina] will be between liberalism and populism."[33]

Onganía's remarks suggested that the government's political base was narrowing dangerously; meanwhile, the opposition was gaining in breadth and also in unity. A multiparty alliance made up of the five major opposition parties in coalition—Peronists, Radicals, Christian Democrats, Intransigents, and the Movement of Integration and Development[34]—was formed in December 1980, to protest repressive measures by the government and the latter's evident lack of enthusiasm for accelerating the transition. The alliance staged anti-government demonstrations throughout 1981, normally ending in

[32] The estimate is uncertain due to the large number of para-statals in Argentina, and also many private enterprises that depend heavily upon government subsidies, minority stock ownership, or unusual tariffs or concessions.

[33] FBIS—*LAT*, January 11, 1982. Dr. Alemann told me in November 1982, after he was no longer in office, that he had taken the Ministry of Economy only on the specific promise of General Galtieri to support him to the hilt on such unpopular measures as the denationalization of the petrochemical and gas industries. When the war began—much to Alemann's surprise, since like most civilian ministers, he knew nothing of inter-service military planning—he rushed to Galtieri and said, "What is this going to do to our plans to reduce the deficit?" He recalled Galtieri assuring him "You let me get the Malvinas back. Once I do, I'll be strong enough to push through your economic reforms—nobody in the military will dare oppose me then!"

[34] Later joined by the Communists and several factions of the Socialist party.

many arrests. The economic crisis now gave it a new issue around which to organize its activities.

On March 30, 1981, the largest protest since 1976 was staged in Buenos Aires and other cities. It was endorsed by the Peronist General Confederation of Labor, but drew upon militants of all opposition parties. Police used tear gas, rubber bullets, water cannon, and at least in one instance, live ammunition to disperse the crowds. Two thousand were arrested in the capital alone; one person was killed by gunfire. Before the political fallout could work itself completely through the political system, the country found itself at war.

The crucial turning point in the history of the regime, however, was a palace coup on December 11, 1981. President Viola, recovering from a mild heart attack, was suddenly and unceremoniously replaced by army commander General Leopoldo F. Galtieri. By this act the army shattered the institutional structure to which all branches of the armed forces had agreed in 1976. Presumably, the price exacted by the navy for this act was the decision to recover the Malvinas (Falkland) Islands,[35] an archipelago off the country's South Atlantic coast seized by Great Britain in the early nineteenth century and held tenaciously ever since. Continued Argentine efforts to reach a negotiated solution had gotten nowhere, possibly because the British had no intention of surrendering sovereignty, which was the only outcome that successive governments in Buenos Aires could accept.[36]

The change of presidents was viewed in Washington with some bemusement, but in Argentina it was interpreted as having important implications for the bilateral relationship. Unlike Viola, Galtieri had lived in the United States as a student officer; along the way he had acquired a sort of English, and a genuine enthusiasm for the American way of life, or rather, what he thought it to be.[37] "On his recent trip to the United States, before he became president," the *Buenos Aires Herald* commented, "General Galtieri either received a much better press or was much more amicably embraced by top U.S. officials than was General Roberto Viola when the latter made a similar trip in early 1980."[38] Since nothing is known of the substance of the dis-

[35] This was the judgment of U.S. Secretary of State Alexander M. Haig, Jr., in all probability based upon fairly authoritative information. See his *Caveat: Reagan Realism and Foreign Policy* (New York: Macmillan, 1984).

[36] The discussions had gone on, more or less fitfully, for many years. The basic division was this: the Argentines regarded the status of the islands as a matter of decolonization; the British, of self-determination. Both were right. The British wanted the 2,000 islanders, who are mostly descendants of Scotch and Irish farmers and shepherds, to be allowed to determine their own future, which inevitably meant to remain a dependency of Great Britain. The Argentines basically addressed the issue as if the islands were unoccupied; had they so been, there would have been no question that the decolonization criterion would have decisively favored their case.

[37] Ambassador Kirkpatrick mentioned to me in a conversation in early 1982 that Galtieri left her with the impression that he liked the United States so much that "he would like to live here," a fairly astounding thing for an Argentine general to say.

[38] FBIS—*LAT*, January 11, 1982.

cussions between Galtieri and the Pentagon on that trip, one can only speculate on why he might be so treated, if in fact he was. Since the general was intoxicated much of the time,[39] it is possible that he had little notion of the nuances of what was being said to him, or the meaning behind what might have been nothing more than ceremonial courtesies. Whatever the facts, Galtieri regarded himself as having a special relationship with the Reagan administration. It was this, evidently, that encouraged him to seize power, and that probably contributed to his decision to embark upon a desperate military adventure in the South Atlantic.

[39] Evidence to me by several U.S. senior military officials present at various functions.

Argentina
Goes to War

On April 2, 1982, an Argentine expeditionary force occupied the Falkland (Malvinas) Islands, a windswept archipelago in the South Atlantic that has formed the object of nationalist sentiment on the Argentine mainland for more than a hundred years. Galtieri's military adventure took the Reagan administration totally by surprise. Nonetheless, many Argentines then and later speculated that, given Washington's supposedly close relationship with the Galtieri regime, it *must* have known, if indeed not specifically approved, of the junta's plans.

They argued, for example, that the highest U.S. authorities could not possibly have been ignorant of several important signals, such as the arbitrary extension of the tour of the current conscript class, or certain highly unusual military movements on the ground. Moreover, they pointed out that the U.S. chief of naval operations, Admiral Thomas Hayward, was in Buenos Aires on an official visit at the time. Actually, U.S. intelligence did pick up the extraordinary concentration of military vehicles at Comodoro Rivadavia, the Patagonian port from which the Argentine troops were debarked to the islands. But having never seriously considered an invasion as a concrete possibility, the Pentagon and the Central Intelligence Agency failed to "process" that and other relevant information in a way that led to the proper conclusion.[1] As for Admiral Hayward, when asked after the war about possible U.S. collusion in the operation, he merely replied, "We aren't that sophisticated, but then again, we aren't that stupid, either."[2]

As Haig himself later said, the United States "had not paid a great deal of attention to the Falklands situation."[3] It had, however, expended considerable attention on Central America. Galtieri ap-

[1] This is a common problem in intelligence analysis. Information in and of itself without a proper contextual matrix is almost useless. On this subject, see Ernest R. May, ed., *Knowing Your Enemy* (Princeton, N.J.: Princeton University Press, 1986).

[2] Remark at the Washington conference for executives sponsored by the Council of the Americas, June, 1982.

[3] Alexander M. Haig, Jr., *Caveat: Reagan Realism and Foreign Policy* (New York: Macmillan, 1984), p. 262.

parently imagined that Argentine assistance in that area would be sufficient to persuade the United States to give him a free hand in the South Atlantic. He even insinuated as much to the U.S. ambassador in Buenos Aires, Harry Shlaudeman, once his troops had landed, and waved aside all the envoy's protests to the contrary.[4] As Haig later put it, the junta displayed "a pattern typical of many militarized, authoritarian, and xenophobic regimes." It imagined that it could get away with retaking the Malvinas "because Britain was weak and the United States was corrupt."[5] Within less than a month, the Argentine generals would discover they had been wrong on both counts.

Galtieri had not miscalculated on one point, however: the United States did not want to be forced to choose between two allies—one old, one new—and would do everything possible to prevent a war between them.[6] As it was, President Reagan spent nearly an hour on the phone trying without success to convince Galtieri to call off the invasion.[7] On April 6 he ordered Haig to travel to London and Buenos Aires to see if some kind of *démarche* could be arranged.

Haig immediately embarked upon a diplomatic odyssey extraordinary even in the age of jet travel. Moving between Washington, London, and Buenos Aires, largely at night, he was forced to change biological clocks, seasons, languages, and political and cultural contexts several times. In London, British prime minister Margaret Thatcher expressed an iron determination not to reward aggression, as some of her predecessors had done in the 1930s; she also affirmed her readiness to take whatever military action necessary to defend the islanders' rights to self-determination.

In Buenos Aires, the prospects of a compromise were even more remote: during Haig's progress from the airport into the city, he was assailed by vociferous, chanting crowds of Argentines demanding their place in the sun, a spectacle which, the secretary later wrote, reminded him of newsreels of fascist Italy. More to the point, Haig almost immediately grasped the degree to which Galtieri, although the nominal head of the Argentine government, was not a free agent. Behind him lurked not only the other service chiefs, notably Admiral Jorge Anaya, but also corps and division commanders of the Argentine army, all presumably as ambitious for his job as Galtieri himself had once been for Viola's, and watching for any misstep that might be

---

[4] Ibid., pp. 275-76.

[5] Ibid., p. 267.

[6] Such a war, Haig wrote, "would drive Galtieri from office and perhaps inflict something worse on Argentina and the Americas." This was the conventional wisdom of the time, not only in Washington but also in many circles within Argentina itself. Ibid., p. 271.

[7] At one point in the conversation, Galtieri is supposed to have told Reagan that it was "too late" in any case. It was. The Argentine strongman refused to take Reagan's call until the first troops landed in the archipelago.

used against him if he failed to produce a glorious victory at the conference.[8]

Haig engaged in several enervating negotiating sessions with Galtieri, Foreign Minister Nicanor Costa Méndez, and their staffs, only to reach agreements that were repudiated by their signators within a matter of hours. It became clear, the secretary later wrote, "that I was not dealing with people who were in a position to negotiate in good faith." Every accord had to be vetted by an informal parliament of generals and admirals; each one failed to meet with their approval. When it became clear that the Argentines were not going to yield an inch, Haig told them frankly that it meant war. To this Galtieri could only whimper to Ambassador Shlaudeman, "I do not understand why the United States, with all of its resources, cannot stop Margaret Thatcher from launching this attack."[9]

Though the British had originally agreed to Haig's mediation, Mrs. Thatcher had insisted on mounting an expeditionary force composed of the Royal Navy, army commandoes, and the Royal Marines in the event of his failure. Assembled in record time, it sailed from Plymouth on April 5. Twenty-three days later, on April 28, it established a sea blockade of the islands and began landing commando parties on their western coast. On June 12 and 13 the British advanced on Port Stanley (Puerto Argentino), the capital of the archipelago, and on June 14, the commander of the Argentine expeditionary force and military governor of the islands, General Mario Menéndez, surrendered to his British counterpart.[10]

Haig had warned the Argentines when he began the mediation that if a compromise could not be reached, that the United States would be obliged to come down on the side of Great Britain,[11] which it did on April 30. At the same time, the United States announced that it would withhold certification of Argentine eligibility for military sales, Eximbank credits and guarantees, and loans from the Commodity Credit Corporation. In other words, starting from very different points, operating under very different assumptions and in different contexts, both the Carter and Reagan administrations ended up with roughly the same Argentine policy.

The U.S. decision to support Great Britain came as a shock and surprise not only to Galtieri and the junta, but to the Argentine man in the street as well. There was much talk of "betrayal," though precisely why a narrow and partial alliance scarcely two years old should supplant one that went back to 1917, tested in two world wars

---

[8] Haig, *Caveat*, pp. 271-80.

[9] Ibid., p. 292.

[10] Of the many books dealing with the war, probably the best is *The Sunday Times* of London Insight Team, *War in the Falklands: The Full Story* (New York: Harper and Row, 1982).

[11] Haig, *Caveat*, p. 295.

and consolidated by deep cultural and political affinities, was never explained. Indeed, up to the morning of April 2, 1982, most Argentines would probably have denied vociferously that their country was an ally of the United States at all. Nonetheless, feelings against the United States ran high, indeed higher than against the British themselves.[12]

Haig's tilt in favor of the British totally altered the diplomatic situation in Buenos Aires. The Galtieri government overnight discovered that Argentina was a member of the Third World, and that its closest allies within the hemisphere were Latin American nations like Venezuela and Peru, who for reasons of their own supported Buenos Aires's claim to the islands. The ambassadors of Cuba and the Soviet Union suddenly became frequent visitors to the Foreign Ministry, the former for the first time since the overthrow of Isabel Perón. In early June, Galtieri dispatched Foreign Minister Costa Méndez to Havana to attend a meeting of the Non-Aligned Movement, where he signed a $100 million trade agreement with the Cubans, and spoke of the United States in vituperative terms exceptional even for that forum; indeed, many Asian and African delegates to the meeting were reportedly surprised "at the unusually radical stance [he] adopted . . . on numerous Third World issues."[13]

The war had a serious impact upon the texture of Argentine public life as well. First, though the taking of the islands came as a total surprise to the Argentine public, once the news reached the mainland the result was a widespread, indeed unprecedented euphoria. Thus Galtieri, who had been subject to jeers and catcalls in his public appearances a few weeks before,[14] was now the idol of the Argentine masses, and his appearances on the balcony of Government House, overlooking the Plaza de Mayo, began to resemble similar events during the reign of General Perón.

Second, since the Malvinas claim was one of the major set-pieces of Argentine nationalism, all of the leaders of the opposition, including the Communists, felt obligated to endorse the government's position, and there was a decided muting of criticism of the military regime. For several weeks "politics" in Argentina simply ceased to exist. This had the effect of encouraging the military to hold out for a favorable outcome, regardless of the difficulties.[15] At the same time, it was a

[12] Much to the delight of the Argentine British community, which imagined that it might somehow now recover the ground it had lost to the Americans since World War II.

[13] *The New York Times*, June 5, 1982.

[14] FBIS—*LAT*, February 2, 1982.

[15] One version that a high-ranking Argentine diplomat shared with me at the time was this: Galtieri originally planned to invade the islands only to bring international attention to Britain's refusal to seriously negotiate their future. Once international pressures had forced the British to the conference table, the Argentines were to have withdrawn their troops pending the outcome of a treaty that would somehow restore their sovereignty. What happened, the diplomat explained, was that popular reaction in Argentina exceeded all expectations, and

double-edged sword, since failure would inevitably benefit the op-position.[16]

Third, the fact that the secretary of state of the United States would leave Washington to "triangulate" between Buenos Aires, London, and his own capital in an attempt to reach a settlement acceptable to them led many Argentines to believe that their country had finally been accorded the international importance it deserved; this was deeply gratifying to a proud, talented people that had suffered many blows to its self-esteem over the past two generations.

Fourth and finally, although there was no serious censorship of war news (in the sense that alternative sources of information were always readily available), Argentines steadfastly believed that they were winning the war until the evening of June 15, 1982, when General Galtieri appeared on television to announce the surrender of Puerto Argentino.[17] This made the shock of reality all the more traumatic. When the president failed to appear as usual on the balcony of Government House after his speech, the mood in the square turned ugly, and tear gas was used to disburse the crowds. Two days later, on June 17, Galtieri resigned, to be replaced by a provisional government pledged to hold elections. Argentina's longest and most violent experience with military government had come to an end.

Galtieri felt obligated to discard his relatively prudent scenario, persisting in the occupation, and therefore on the road to war.

[16] As Haig writes, "the junta, in its most mulish moments, was in touch with civilian politicians as well as military officers. All three members of the junta complained, throughout their conversations with me, that it was unjust that the military should have to deal in this way with a political question. The harshness, the unyielding position on the question of sovereignty, I was told later, came not from the military, but from some of the civilian political parties, and most especially the Peronists." (*Caveat*, p. 295.) This may not have been technically true, but no doubt it expressed the deepest fears of the junta.

[17] Foreign newspapers and magazines were available in Buenos Aires throughout the war, and Uruguayan and Chilean radio, drawing upon Reuters and other European and U.S. news agencies, were able to provide Argentine listeners with accurate and up-to-date information on the military action in the archipelago. But Argentines simply preferred to believe their own government, or the government-controlled press. It is an interesting example of mass delusion and deserves further investigation by students of the subject.

Conclusions and
Some Might-Have-Beens

In October 1983, the military government called elections, and the winner was Radical Raúl Alfonsín, a courageous, independent politician who was anathema not only to the armed forces, but also to the Peronist party and the Roman Catholic hierarchy. It was the first time in many years that genuinely competitive elections were held in Argentina, entirely free of proscriptions; it was also the first time the Peronists were forced to run someone other than their founder for the presidency.[1] Most important of all, it was the first time that the Peronists had ever lost a presidential election; Alfonsín's victory dealt a crushing blow to the notion of the inevitability and, indeed, invincibility that had been part of the movement's mystique for two generations.

In the United States, Alfonsín's victory was interpreted according to philosophical preferences or partisan interests. The Reagan administration was quick to claim credit for Argentina's return to democracy, which under the circumstances was very wide of the mark. But having gambled on the junta and failed, it graciously accepted the outcome, and prepared to work with Galtieri's successors. Reagan's domestic critics were frankly ecstatic at the defeat not only of the armed forces but of the Peronists as well, and seized upon Alfonsín's victory as proof that positive political forces had always lurked just below the surface, and that their late emergence was due to a mean-spirited refusal by the White House to recognize their existence all along.[2] It was difficult to argue with success, however, and with Alfonsín's inauguration in December 1983, there was no means with which the human rights community and the left in Congress and outside of it could continue to use Argentina as a stick to beat the Reagan administration's Latin American policy.

In Argentina itself, the United States was viewed at best with profound ambivalence at all points along the political spectrum. For the opposition and the human rights community, Washington still

---

[1] Or someone obviously standing in for him, as in the case of Héctor Cámpora.
[2] Peter D. Bell, "Democracy and Double Standards," *World Policy Journal*, Fall 1985, pp. 711-30.

represented the same forces that were prepared to do business with the junta, and was, therefore, a country both feared and hated. At the same time, however, for the Radical party and Alfonsín in particular, who inherited a country defeated militarily and shattered economically, there was no choice but to accept Reagan's outstretched hand of friendship and hope for the best.

Meanwhile, Washington's local allies in the armed forces and the extreme right, cruelly disillusioned by their abandonment in the South Atlantic war, revived ancient grudges and nourished them anew. Some re-emerging political figures, like Adolfo Gass, chairman of the Argentine Senate Foreign Relations Committee, managed to have it both ways; damning the United States for originally supporting the junta, but also for not supporting it during the war with Great Britain, ignoring the most evident and obvious relationship between events and outcomes.[3]

For most Argentine political figures, however, the obvious lesson of the war was the need to repair relations with the United States. Among other things, this meant not dwelling excessively on embarrassing details of recent history, a posture that meshed perfectly with the needs of the Reagan administration as well.

Though perhaps a bit too opportunistic, the Argentine penchant for starting over with a clean slate had at least the advantage of putting the U.S. role in a more accurate perspective. Between 1977 and 1982, U.S. objectives there changed, as did the situation on the ground, but—contrary to what many domestic critics of the Reagan administration continued to hold—it is doubtful that American pressures one way or the other had much to do with the outcome, except in unintended ways.

During the Carter period, a principled human rights policy had virtues of its own, but did not play a major role in staying the hand of the junta. On the other hand, had Washington attempted during those years to do "business as usual"—as some urged it to do—when thousands of innocent people were being tortured and killed, it would have produced a new and even more lurid crop of myths about the CIA, covert action, and the military-industrial complex. (As it was, the report of the National Commission on Disappeared Persons, *Nunca más* [1985], attributed the savage anti-communism of the Argentine armed forces to the "national security doctrine" supposedly taught them at the School of the Americas in Panama and at service schools in the continental United States.)

By keeping its distance from the junta in the blackest period of its rule, the Carter administration preserved the good name of the United States in the eventuality of a return to democratic rule. The

---

[3] Conversation with Senator Adolfo Gass, Caracas, Venezuela, June 1986.

fact that some Argentines today choose to give the Carter administration more credit than it may in fact deserve is not necessarily a bad thing for bilateral relations as a whole. The truth is that by couching the issue of human rights in such stringently moralistic terms, the Carter administration made it difficult to reward progress, since the only forward movement in Argentina that could satisfy its own criteria and that of its human rights constituency was highly unlikely in the short term—namely, the self-liquidation of the military regime and its replacement by an elected civilian administration. This might have happened eventually, but not, surely, to please the United States. Had it occurred within the framework of *concertación*, it would have been a democracy flawed from birth.[4]

To be sure, a more flexible, responsive policy on the part of the Carter people probably would not have made much of a difference either. This much was proven by the Reagan administration, which in 1981 hastened to recognize the changed situation, and to reward the Argentine government accordingly. While the junta expressed satisfaction and even delight with this turn of events, it saw no particular reason to go any further or faster toward political devolution because of it, and even modest pressures from the United States (on the matter of "disappearances") were sharply turned aside. Even the area of greatest agreement with the United States, Central American policy, was a matter of convergence rather than outright quid pro quo bargaining. As we have seen, in most areas of real importance to it, the Argentine government went its own way.

Had the United States under a second Carter administration chosen to continue the same exclusionary policy of 1977-1980 throughout 1981 and 1982, it is doubtful the Argentine regime would have responded more favorably, or have disappeared any faster. It is just possible that things would have turned out less well than they did.

No doubt the economic crisis would have provoked the same political unrest, but that might only have accelerated moves toward *concertación* between the armed forces and the more unscrupulous elements of the Peronist party. As it was, encouraged by Washington's gestures, and deluded (under Galtieri) that it had some sort of blank check from the United States, Argentina chose to meet its domestic political crisis with a diversionary military expedition in the South Atlantic. The effect was to discredit the armed forces in their narrow professional mission and deprive them of their last shreds of prestige in the civilian community. This was precisely the precondition to the

---

[4] Even the Alfonsín administration, rigorously adhering to due process, subsequently found it politically and juridically impossible to fix proper responsibility for atrocities during the military period. One need only speculate on the possible damage to Argentine institutions had a civilian government come to power in 1983 or later with a prearranged "gentleman's agreement" with the military.

establishment—one can hardly say "the restoration"—of a viable democratic alternative in Argentina.

Had Argentina been closer, poorer, smaller, and more dependent upon U.S. markets and sources of supply, presumably U.S. leverage and influence would have been greater. But, as the case of Somoza's Nicaragua demonstrates, so would the countervailing influences within the Washington policy community. In that eventuality, sanctions might never have been applied in the first place. As it was, the mix of distance, uncertain geopolitical importance, and competitive economies made U.S. policy largely a chimera—a psychological game played with mirrors, in which the perception of American support (for the opposition under Carter, for the junta under Reagan) was supposed to acquire a force of its own, but never quite did. Carter could not depose the junta, and Reagan could not save it; neither Wilsonian idealism nor *Realpolitik* could alter the peculiar logic that dictated the eventual turn of Argentine events.

INDEX

Afghanistan, 4
Agriculture, Department of, 23
Aja Espil, Jorge A., 45
Alfonsín, Raúl, 5, 35n, 40, 55
Algeria, 26
Alemann, Roberto, 46
Allende, Salvador, 5
Allende government, 18
Alliance for Progress, 7
Allis-Chalmers, 27n
Amnesty International, 27, 32, 34
Anaya, Admiral Jorge, 50
anti-Americanism, 4
anti-communism, 5, 17, 20
anti-Semitism, 20
Arendt, Hannah, 37
Argentine-American Alliance (1982), 42, 45
Argentine Anti-Communist Alliance (Triple A), 15
Argentine Communist party, 10, 21n
Argentine Senate Foreign Relations Committee, 56
arms embargo, 30, 32

Balbín, Ricardo, 13
Barnes, Michael, 31, 32
Bonker, Dan, 32, 33
Brazil, 38, 44n
Brzezinski, Zbigniew, 22, 23
Buenos Aires 1, 11, 14

Cambio, 41
Camilión, Oscar, 39, 44, 45
Camp David Accords, 44
Cámpora, Héctor J., 11n, 13, 14, 55n
Canada, 22
Carter administration, 17, 19, 22, 23, 27, 29, 34, 35, 43, 51, 57
Carter, Jimmy, 4, 18, 20n, 22
Castro, Fidel, 5, 12
Catholic Church, 13
Central Intelligence Agency (CIA), 49, 56

Chile, 4, 20, 22, 28, 33
Colombia, 43
Commodity Credit Corporation, 51
Comodoro Rivadavia, 49
Communist(s), 10, 12, 52
concertación, 40, 41, 57
Conservative party, 9
Conservatives, 9, 10, 40
constitution, Argentine (1853), 3
Continental Treaty (1856), 4
continuísmo, 40
convicción, 41
Costa Méndez, Nicanor, 44, 51, 52
Cuba, 5, 12, 52

Defense Department, 22
Deolindo Bittel, Felipe, 16, 40
Derian, Patricia, 17, 18, 20, 24
de Rivera, Primo, 12
"Dictatorships and Double Standards,' 29n, 37
"dirty war," 16, 21, 41, 43
"disappearances," 16, 21, 38, 41, 57
Dominican Republic, 7, 11
Duarte de Perón, Eva, 9

Eastern Airlines, 1
Ecuador, 4
Eldridge, Joseph (Washington Office on Latin America), 32
El Salvador, 43, 45
Enders, Thomas, 44
European Economic Community, 2
Eximbank, 51

Falkland Islands (Malvinas), 47, 49
Faustino Sarmiento, Domingo, 3
Feeney, Patricia, 32
Fenwick, Milicent, 33
First World War, 2
Ford administration, 19
Fracassi, Eduardo, 41

59

France, 23; French, 3
Frondizi, Arturo, 6, 7, 11

Galtieri, Leopoldo, 39, 44, 45, 47-53, 55, 57
Gass, Adolfo, 56
General Confederation of Labor, 47
Germans, 3
Government House, 52
Goodpaster, Andrew, 23, 24
grain embargo, 4, 23, 32
Great Britain, 1, 4, 47, 51
Guatemala, 28
Guineau-Bissau, 20

habeas corpus, 16, 38n
Haig, Alexander M., Jr., 28, 49-52
Haiti, 28
Hannum, Hurst, 34
Harkin, Tom, 34
Hayward, Thomas, 49
Hodges, Luther H., 27n
Honduras, 43n
human rights, 17, 19, 21, 24, 27, 28 ,29
Humphrey-Kennedy Amendment, 21
    22, 31, 32, 34, 35

Illia, Arturo, 6, 7
Inter-American Treaty of Reciprocal
    Assistance (Rio Pact), 5
International Security and Develop-
    ment Cooperation Act (1980):Section
    725, 35
Iraq, 20, 44n
"Isabel," 14, 15
Iscaro, Rubens, 21n
isolationism, 3, 4
Israel, 22, 42, 43
Italians, 1

Jackson, Henry, 19n
Japan, 22
Johnson, Ernest B., Jr., 34
Justicialist party, 11

Karth, James E., 32
Kirkpatrick, Jeane J., 29n, 37, 44, 45,
    47n
Kissinger, Henry A., 21

LaFalce, John J., 34
Lanusse, Alejandro, 5
Lastiri, Raul, 13, 14
Lawyers Committee on Human Rights
    (New York), 32, 33, 42
Lefever, Ernest, 30, 31

Lewis, Anthony, 31
Lima, 1
Lipset, Seymour Martin, 37
López Rega, José, 15

Madrid, 11, 12
Malvinas (Falklands), 46n, 47, 49, 50,
    52
Martinez de Perón, María Estela, 14,
    15, 17, 40, 52
Marxism, 12
Massera, Eduardo, 40, 41, 46
masserista, 41
Menéndez, Mario, 51, 52
mercantilism, 23-24
Mexico, 10, 43
Mica, Dan, 33
militarism, 20
monetarism, 20
Moscow, 1
Moynihan, Daniel Patrick, 31
Multilateral lending (PL95-118), 34
Muskie, Edmund, 24
Mussolini, Benito, 12

National Commission on Disappeared
    Persons, 56
National Democratic party, 9
National Directorate of Military Facto-
    ries (DNFM), 22
National Guard, 43
Neumann, Siegfried, 37
neutralism, 3, 20
Nicaragua, 5, 11, 20, 43, 58; civil war,
    42
Nixon administration, 19
Non-aligned Movement, 52
Nunca Mas (1985), 56

Onganía, Juan Carlos, 46
Organization of American States, 43

Panama, 4, 20n
Panama Conference of the Pan-Ameri-
    can Union, 5
Paraguay, 11, 33
Partido Revolucionario Institicional
    (PRI), 10
partido unico, 10
PEN (Poder Ejecutivo Nacional), 38
Pentagon, 48, 49
Perón, Juan, 5, 6, 11, 12
Peronism, 9, 12, 13; Peronists, 40, 55
Peru, 4
Peyser, Peter, 23n
Philippines, 20
Pinochetism, 21n

PL95-118 (1977) (Multilateral lending), 34
Port Stanley (Puerto Argentino), 51
Puerto Argentino (Port Stanley), 53

Quijano, Raúl, 45

Radical party, 6, 13, 40
Radicals, 10, 40
Reagan administration, 29, 35, 41, 43, 55-57
Reagan, Ronald 37, 50, 51
Realpolitik, 21, 58
Rio Pact (Inter-American Treaty of Reciprocal Assistance), 5
Romania, 20

Sandinista, 43
Schell, Orville (Lawyers Committee on Human Rights [New York]), 32, 33, 42
School of the Americas, 56
Second World War, 2, 4, 10, 11
Shlaudeman, Harry, 50, 51
Sinai Peace Force, 44
"sixth dominion," 2
Social Democratic party, 4
Socialists, 10
Somalia, 20
Somoza Debayle, Anastasio, 42, 58
South Africa, 22, 43
South Korea, 20n, 43
Soviet Union, 23, 52
Spain, 11; Spaniards, 1
State Department, 20, 21, 25, 44
Subcommittee on International Development, Institutions and Finance, 33
Swift and Company, 3
Syria, 20

Taiwan, 22, 43
Takacs, Esteban, 44
terror, 15, 28
Thatcher, Margaret, 50, 51
Theberge, James D., 32, 33, 38
Timerman, Jacobo, 21, 30
Tosco, Augusto, 14
Treasury Department, 33
Triple A (Argentine Anti-Communist Alliance), 15

U.N. Commission on Human Rights, 5, 21
United States, 1, 2, 4, 22
United States Export-Import Bank, 27n
Uruguay, 28, 33

Vance, Cyrus, 19
Venezuela, 11, 43, 52
Vezza, Alfredo, 41
Videla, Jorge, 16, 34
Vietnam War, 18, 19
Viola, Roberto, 16, 30, 33, 39, 45-48, 50

Watergate, 18
Western Europe, 2, 3
West Germany, 22
Westinghouse, 27n
Whitaker, Arthur P., 4n, 6, 7n
Wilsonian idealism, 58

Yankeephobia, 3, 7
Young, Andrew, 17
Yrigoyen, Hipólito, 10
Yugoslavia, 20

FOREIGN POLICY RESEARCH INSTITUTE

 Founded in 1955, the Foreign Policy Research Institute is an independent, publicly supported, nonprofit organization devoted to the public dissemination of scholarly research affecting the national interests of the United States. As a catalyst for the exchange of ideas, FPRI seeks to shape the climate in which American foreign policy is made. Research is conducted by the FPRI's staff, supplemented by the work of Fellows and Associate Scholars.

In addition to *The Philadelphia Papers*, the Foreign Policy Research Institute publishes ORBIS, a quarterly journal of world affairs. The *FPRI Book Series* includes volumes on the cutting edge of research.

FPRI administers the *Inter-University Seminar on Foreign Affairs*, which regularly brings together scholars and businessmen for lectures, seminars, and workshops on international issues. Each year the Institute sponsors a competition for the *Thornton D. Hooper Fellowship in International Affairs;* the Hooper Fellow spends a year in residence at FPRI conducting independent research. The FPRI *Internship Program* provides opportunities for students who are contemplating a career in international affairs.

All contributions to the Institute are tax-deductible.

The Philadelphia Papers

Editors: ADAM M. GARFINKLE and DANIEL PIPES
Managing Editor: ROGER S. DONWAY
Manuscript Editor: JOANN TOMAZINIS
Assistant Editor: MARK W. POWELL

BOARD OF EDITORS

The Philadelphia Papers

The Foreign Policy Research Institute publishes *The Philadelphia Papers* on an occasional basis to focus on specific aspects of world affairs. Topics include the social and cultural bases of politics, military strategy, technology and arms control, problems of war and unconventional conflict, international economics, and diplomacy.

Each *Philadelphia Paper* deals with a single topic at a length between that of an article and a book. Essays address foreign-policy issues of contemporary relevance with an eye to policy issues facing Americans and the United States government. Submissions are welcome.

Opinions expressed in this series are those of the authors alone.

BACK TITLES IN PRINT

Muriel Atkin, **The Subtlest Battle: Islam In Soviet Tajikistan**, 1989. 66 pp. $8.00.

Adam M. Garfinkle, **The Politics of the Nuclear Freeze**, 1984. 258 pp. $7.95.

Colin S. Gray, **Nuclear Strategy and Strategic Planning**, 1984. 130 pp. $5.95.

Robert F. Turner, **The War Powers Resolution: Its Implementation in Theory and Practice**, with a foreword by Senator John Tower, 1983. 147 pp. $4.95.

Shaheen Ayubi, Richard Bissell, et al., **Economic Sanctions in U.S. Foreign Policy**, 1982. 86 pp. $3.95.

Staff of the Foreign Policy Research Institute, **The Three Percent Solution and the Future of NATO**, 1981. 118 pp. $6.95.

Harvey Sicherman, **Broker or Advocate: The U.S. Role in the Arab-Israeli Dispute, 1973-1978**, 1979. 120 pp. $5.95.

Nimrod Novik, **On the Shores of Bab al-Mandab: Soviet Diplomacy and Regional Dynamics**, 1979. 83 pp. $3.95.

Adam M. Garfinkle, **"Finlandization": A Map to a Metaphor**, 1978. 56 pp. $3.95.